D1229907

Doomed in Afghanistan

Doomed in Afghanistan

A UN Officer's Memoir of the Fall of Kabul and Najibullah's Failed Escape, 1992

Phillip Corwin

Rutgers University Press

New Brunswick, New Jersey, and London

Library of Congress Cataloging-in-Publication Data
Corwin, Phillip.
Doomed in Afghanistan : a UN officer's memoir of the fall of Kabul
and Najibullah's failed escape, 1992 / Phillip Corwin.
p. cm.
Includes bibliographical references and index.
ISBN 0-8135-3171-3 (alk. paper)
1. Afghanistan—History—Soviet occupation, 1979–1989—Personal
narratives. 2. Najib, 1947– . 3. United Nations—Afghanistan.
4. Corwin, Phillip. I. Title.

DS371.3 .C67 2003
958.104'6—dc21   2002024831

British Cataloging-in-Publication information is available from the
British Library.

Manufactured in the United States of America

O piteous spectacle! O bloody times!
Whiles lions war and battle for their dens,
Poor harmless lambs abide their enmity.

    William Shakespeare, 3 *Henry VI*, (II, v)

Contents

Preface

This story begins on a wintry morning in March 1992, when a colleague in the United Nations approached me to ask if I would be interested in going on an urgent mission to Afghanistan.

Afghanistan! I knew very little about the country. Beautiful carpets, empyrean mountains, vast deserts, and a people legendary for their resistance to colonizers. People who could be both sentimental and fierce. A nation of traders and warriors that had resisted the great British armies of the nineteenth century and only recently had repelled the great armies of the Soviet Union.

I would gladly have gone to Afghanistan for no reason at all. Just to learn, to view, to add perspective to my understanding of the world. And to take a break from the urbanized existence of a New York City office, as much as I loved Manhattan. But here, I realized immediately, was an opportunity that was more than frivolous or fortuitous. Here was an opportunity to go to an exotic country, not as a tourist, but as part of a United Nations peacekeeping mission, a mission no doubt intended to help relieve the suffering of a population that was in deep pain.

It was almost as if I had no choice. I had to go to Afghanistan. How could I not go? Before I even knew the details of the assignment, how long it would last, or what dangers it might entail, I knew I would go, that I had to go. A magnet in the clouds over the Hindu Kush was drawing me there.

And I knew more. I knew that in the days before I left New York I would contact every Afghan I knew and meet with as many as possible, pick their brains, take notes, and learn every fact I could. And I would read, read, read about Afghanistan—novels, maps, newspaper articles, histories. I also suspected that if the mission were urgent, I would probably be leaving within a few weeks.

My colleague had said I should call him by the end of the day to tell him of my decision. It took me an hour to decide. I said *yes*.

––––––––

The centerpiece of this book is the aborted escape of Afghan president Najibullah[1] (also known as Najib) from his home in the middle of the night on 15–16 April 1992. I was in the UN convoy that tried to take him to the airport and fly him into exile in New Delhi, and I was in the team that had to deal with the aftermath of that frustrated effort. Najib's resignation of the presidency and his departure from Afghanistan had been intended to end the ongoing civil war there and clear the way for a peaceful coalition to succeed him. No one to my knowledge has written a detailed account of his attempted evacuation or of the frenzied negotiations before and after that tried to forestall the avaricious demons of anarchy and chaos. That is one reason, perhaps the major reason, for writing this book: to provide a firsthand account of a critical event that will interest any curious reader, and at the same time will provide a primary research document for future historians.

I am also hopeful that this story will augment, perhaps in some cases restore, appreciation and respect for the

agents and processes of diplomacy. None of us in the UN
mission in Kabul in April 1992 had anything to gain mate-
rially from our work. Though some may have had political
agendas that reflected their national interest, I am convinced that at the time we were all motivated by a humanitarian impulse that is hard to describe in the abstract. At
the risk of sounding naïve, I must say that at such times,
the possibility of saving thousands of human lives provides
an incredible emotional high. And although the international community failed to prevent the relentless, merciless
carnage that would follow in Afghanistan, its diplomatic
and humanitarian efforts should not go unacknowledged.
The UN did not start the series of wars there, and it could
not end them. But its efforts came closer to achieving peace
than those of any other factor. Those parties that refused to
abide by international accords were at fault, not the accords
themselves, or the mediators who negotiated them. At best,
the UN's intentions in Afghanistan were always to act, in
the words of Secretary-General Boutros-Ghali, "as a catalyst and a facilitator for the Afghan people themselves to
resolve their differences politically."[2]

In a sense, this book is also an *amicus curiae* to the
court of world opinion that may one day assess responsibility for the devastation of the sovereign state of Afghanistan. We who were there at the time knew very well,
despite our hopes, that we were overmatched and under-
gunned players in another enactment of The Great Game
(the title of a book by Peter Hopkirk, which describes the
nineteenth-century struggle between Great Britain and
Imperial Russia for supremacy in central Asia and led to the
creation of Afghanistan as a buffer state). The antagonists in
1992 were different than before, but the Great Game was
just as lethal, just as strategic. In fact, we were playing on a
field crowded with more powerful and ambitious actors.

And we lost. There can be no doubt of that. But what we lost as representatives of the international community was nothing compared to what the people of Afghanistan lost, and will not recover for decades.

———

Doomed in Afghanistan is divided into five parts. The first chapter deals with the background to my going to Afghanistan and points out similarities between the events in Afghanistan in 1992 and earlier UN peacekeeping operations. These analogies not only give added dimension to the events described in this book but also suggest guidelines for future peacekeeping operations, including in post-Taliban Afghanistan. Chapter 2 is the journal of my experiences, and as such, is the spine of the book. Its entries are for the most part day by day, or every few days, except during the fateful night of 15–16 April, when they are often hour by hour. Chapter 3 is a close textual analysis of documents issued and discussed at United Nations headquarters in New York, related to happenings on the ground in Afghanistan. The analysis shows how to interpret certain "code" words and how diplomats far from the action skew events on the ground in order to attain maximum political advantage. Chapter 4 is an interview more than seven years after Najib's failed escape with two Afghan exiles who were in Afghanistan when I was. Chapter 5 is both retrospective and futuristic. It looks back, after the terror of September 11, 2001, at the significance of the events of 1992, and also attempts to predict what the major problems will be for Afghanistan in the post-Taliban era.

———

The events surrounding Najib's failed flight from Kabul resonate vividly in terms of the UN's role in international peacekeeping, its role in conflicts within a country, its moral and political image, and its exploitation both as a scapegoat and as a haven of last resort. On a different level, these events also have implications for understanding the balance of power in the immediate aftermath of the Cold War, the prerogatives of the office of the secretary-general, and the critical transition of communist states into fledgling democracies. A close examination of the ultimate fate of Najibullah and how he arrived there might even help to understand the turmoil erupting in other developing countries, specifically in the Muslim world. Najib's destiny may not have been a watershed in world history, but it may well have been a touchstone.

Finally, a comment about the style of the journal. The entries are generally in the present tense. Later thoughts I had about them, when recording them, or additional information to clarify the entries, are placed in brackets. Analyses that came after the fact are in a different typestyle. I don't think this style is troublesome. And, after all, as Marshall McLuhan was fond of telling us, knowledge is associative rather than linear.

Acknowledgments

The facts and opinions in this book are solely my responsibility. There are those, however, whom I must thank for their support and encouragement. Without them, this book would not have been possible. To start with, there was Benon Sevan, the secretary-general's personal representative in Afghanistan and Pakistan, who selected me for the assignment that served as the basis for this book. As head of mission, he was indefatigable and dedicated, always giving as much, even more, than he demanded from his staff. On the home front, there were my children, whom I thought of constantly, and whose emotional vitality helped me to endure and at the same time to appreciate the profound tragedy of Afghan children. There is nothing more devastating than the sight of starving and/or brutalized children, and Afghanistan is filled with them. Then there was Dolores Perin, who at the last moment consented to read large parts of this book and made very helpful comments. Finally, there were my collaborators at Rutgers University Press. I am grateful to my editor, David Myers, who made several valuable suggestions, and to the entire Rutgers team that guided the manuscript through the perils of production.

Glossary

Avni Botsali Turkish diplomat, seconded to the United Nations, who served as deputy to Benon Sevan

Boutros Boutros-Ghali Secretary-general of the United Nations

Coalition of the North (a.k.a. the Northern Alliance) Opposition forces made up mainly of Tajiks and Uzbeks and based in the northern part of Afghanistan

Council of Impartials A group of leaders intended to form a transitional authority in the period after Najibullah's resignation, until a government could be installed

Abdul Rashid Dostom Uzbek military commander

Hazara Ethnic group comprising about 19 percent of Afghan population

Gulbuddin Hekmatyar Pashtun military commander supported by Pakistan

Inter-Services Intelligence Directorate (ISI) The intelligence agency of the Pakistan government

Loya Jirga In Afghan tradition, a "grand council" composed of the widest possible group of leaders, convened to resolve national problems, such as intertribal disputes, social reforms, and national legislation

Ahmed Shah Massoud Tajik military commander, a leader of the resistance against the Soviet Union during the 1980s, and later against the Taliban

Mujahidin Opposition forces (literally, people of the Jihad or holy struggle) fighting to overthrow the communist government of President Najibullah. In the early 1990s, there were at least fifteen different factions.

Najibullah President of Afghanistan, 1986–1992

Patrick Nowlan Head of military advisory unit of OSGAP

OSGAP The Office of the Secretary-General in Afghanistan and Pakistan, official title of the United Nations mission in the region

Pashtun Major ethnic group in Afghanistan, comprising about 38 percent of population

Burhanuddin Rabbani Ethnic Tajik, political ally of General Massoud, and leader of Jamaat Islami Party

ASIA AND THE PACIFIC

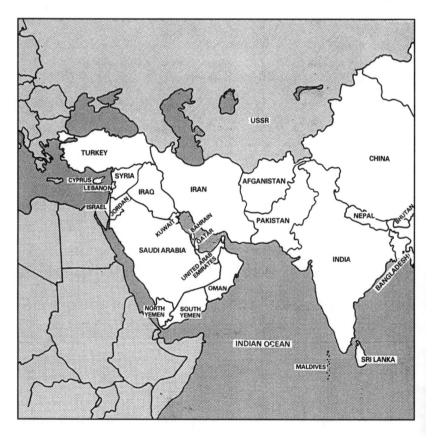

Benon V. Sevan UN secretary-general's personal representative in Afghanistan and Pakistan

Tajik Ethnic group comprising about 25 percent of Afghan population

Turkmen Ethnic group comprising up to 10 percent of Afghan population

Uzbek Ethnic group comprising about 8 percent of Afghan population

Abdul Wakil Minister of foreign affairs of Afghanistan

Watan Party Najibullah's political party, a communist party

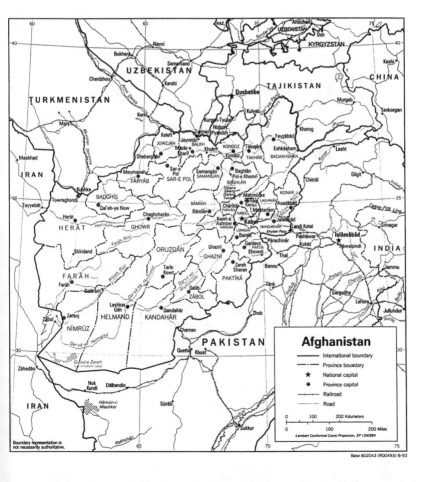

xx

Waiting for the end: Kabul, 4/92

The soldiers smile their smile of pride;
each heart contains a fist inside.
The land they left has gone to seed;
they've learned to shoot but not to read.

In villages with holy names
they've seen the sky explode in flames.
In godly mountains thick with pines
their pets have been deformed by mines.

In playgrounds meant for girls and boys
where lethal pellets lay like toys,
a child that only played at war
has two less fingers than before.

For decades long the *feringhee*
dispatched their best technology
to help the people kill themselves,
then granted aid to fill their shelves.

Now we sit like stumps and wait
as rival armies infiltrate,
as women blot their skin with mud
and stock their cellars with cold food.

My landlord is inured to war,
has seen it many times before.
The only hope, he says, is faith;
the only waste is useless death.
                              —Phillip Corwin

Doomed in Afghanistan

1

Setting

the

Stage

By spring 1992, in accordance with the wishes of the international community and after months of strenuous negotiation, the UN had finally convinced Najibullah to resign his post as president of Afghanistan. All the parties involved in the ongoing civil war there had agreed that there could be no peace until Najib was gone. It was the virtual *sine qua non* for any meaningful colloquy. Accordingly, on 18 March 1992, Najib publicly announced he would resign *as soon as an authority could be designated to replace him*. He did not specify a date for his resignation to be effective; instead, he gave a condition.

Ever since the Soviet Union's withdrawal from Afghanistan in 1989, Najibullah's hold on power had been slipping. For the past few years as many as fifteen different guerrilla groups, known as mujahidin (holy warriors), had been advancing on Kabul, intent on deposing Najib. The mujahidin, armed and financed principally by the United States, Saudi Arabia, and Iran had fought for ten years against the Soviet Union, and once the Soviet Union with-drew they continued their battle against Najib, who had been supported by the Soviet Union. The mujahidin saw Najib as a Soviet puppet, and even worse, as a godless athe-ist ruling a devout Muslim country. They wanted him gone, and refused to include him or his followers in any coalition. Whether the struggle would end once he was gone was a matter of speculation. But it was certain there would be no chance for peace so long as Najib remained in power.

In fact, Najib had lasted much longer that anyone thought he would. The Soviet Union, which had invaded Afghanistan in 1979, had completed its troop pullout in February 1989. Najibullah's communist regime, which had been expected to collapse as soon as Soviet troops left, had held together a disintegrating national structure for another three years. But now the nation seemed about to implode, to plunge into anarchy. The UN, with literally a handful of political officers and a small contingent of military ob-servers, in addition to the humanitarian agencies, was try-ing valiantly to prevent an impending disaster. I wanted to be a part of that effort.

The UN had been negotiating with various opposition leaders to nominate fifteen or twenty names that would take over as an authority to replace Najib. This authority was referred to by either of two names: Council of Impar-tials, or pre-Transition Authority. This Council would hold power until a Loya Jirga could convene to nominate an interim government that would hold power until elections. (Loya Jirga is a Pashto term. Pashto is the language of the Pashtun tribe, the major ethnic group in Afghanistan. Najib was a Pashtun.) To put it another way: The fifteen- to twenty-member council would replace Najib, perhaps for forty-five days, until a Loya Jirga could nominate an interim government. Since the interim government was itself transitional, because it would only serve until elections, the fifteen to twenty members preceding it were called a "pretransition" authority. And since the fifteen to twenty members were supposed to represent *all* the guerrilla groups contending for power, they were considered impartial." Therefore, they were also known as a Council of Impartials.

_____

At the time of my recruitment, I was a member of Secretary-General Boutros Boutros-Ghali's speech writing unit. He had only recently taken office. I had done most of my speechwriting for the previous secretary-general, Javier Pérez de Cuéllar.

Speechwriters do more than write formal speeches. They also prepare personal correspondence, messages, talking points, press statements, and any other communication needed to put forth their client's position on a given issue. As such, they must be aware of the major topics the client has to deal with, and they must be comfortable with diplomats. In certain situations speechwriters actually help formulate policy, since the words they put in the mouth of a client are often policy statements.

There were a number of people in the secretary-general's speech writing unit, but they were not the only ones who prepared texts for the SG. Heads of substantive departments also wrote speeches for the SG. The head of the disarmament division wrote speeches about disarmament. The head of the economic division wrote speeches about economics. And so forth. Our unit tended to write speeches on more general topics. This pattern is true in almost any government or corporate structure. Chief executives simply do not have time to write all their own speeches, personally answer all correspondence, or know every detail about each of the departments for which they speak. They may approve or reject, but seldom do they have the time to draft their own texts.

I must add that I was not the main speechwriter for the SG, although I had written some major speeches. In any case, I had high-level experience dealing with large political issues, and that was one reason I was approached about going to Afghanistan. Another reason was that I'd had high-level experience in previous peacekeeping missions. My last overseas assignment had been as a senior political officer in Western Sahara, where the UN had been trying to organize a referendum to decide the future status of what was once known as the Spanish Sahara. That attempt, still underway a decade later, essentially involved mediation between two bitterly opposed neighbors, Algeria and Morocco. In Afghanistan, as in Western Sahara, ambitious and suspicious neighbors muddied the waters of peace. The practitioners of imperialism generally bequeath a perilous legacy to their successors.

My particular assignment in Afghanistan would be to assist in organizing a Loya Jirga. The UN's idea was to convene the Loya Jirga outside Afghanistan, most likely in Vienna, where better security could be provided than in Kabul, and where all the participants would feel on an equal footing. Kabul was dominated by Pashtun, and leaders of other ethnic groups might feel intimidated or physically threatened there.

The secretary-general envisioned that the Loya Jirga would have "150 middle-level representatives, acceptable to all sides, from all segments of the Afghan people, including representatives of political parties, religious and tribal leaders, opposition groups, resistance commanders, prominent personalities, émigrés and representatives from Kabul."[1] A wide-ranging group, by anyone's standards.

The head of the mission when I arrived in Afghanistan was Benon V. Sevan, who held the title of personal representative of the UN secretary-general in Afghanistan and Pakistan. His title was particularly politicized, as was everything else in the mission.

Ever since the Soviet Union's invasion of Afghanistan on 26 December 1979, the Security Council had been unable to intervene in Afghanistan. The Soviet Union's veto power had prevented the Council from taking action. The Soviet Union maintained that it had been invited into Afghanistan by the legitimate, internationally recognized government (which it had installed), and that the UN Security Council had no authority to intervene in the domestic affairs of a sovereign State. The Soviet Union's position was supported by several other countries, and of course, by Afghanistan.[2]

But a deal was struck, because the situation was urgent, and even those who oppose UN military intervention cannot completely oppose UN involvement. It would mean a loss of international stature for them. And so, as often happens when member states seem at an impasse, they passed the ball to the secretary-general—at the time, Kurt Waldheim. The procedure for this action is circuitous, euphemistic, and virtually unintelligible to all but the initiated, but it sometimes works. At an emergency special session in January 1980, the General Assembly deplored "the recent armed intervention in Afghanistan" and called for the immediate, unconditional, and total withdrawal of "foreign troops" from that country, without saying whose troops they were. Such wording was acceptable to the Soviet Union, which could maintain that other foreign troops—Pakistani, Arab, and Chechen—were in Afghanistan, *un*invited by the recognized government (which they had installed). The Assembly's resolution, which, in

Orwellian doublespeak, could only be recommendatory rather than mandatory as the Security Council's were, included other demands, and, finally, requested the secretary-general to keep Member States and the Security Council informed on progress in implementing the Assembly's resolution. In effect, this last phrase on keeping Member States and the Security Council informed allowed the secretary-general to exercise his authority under a unique concept known as "good offices." This concept, understood but rarely stated, allows the secretary-general to use his ingenuity, and to pursue contacts with parties to a conflict, without the publicity and heavy authority of the Security Council. It does not allow the secretary-general to ignore or contradict the Security Council, but it gives him flexibility. It is one of his most powerful negotiating tools.

After a series of consultations with the concerned parties, Waldheim appointed Javier Pérez de Cuéllar to be his personal representative on the issue. The following year, when Pérez de Cuéllar was elected secretary-general, he appointed Diego Cordovez to the post of personal representative to Afghanistan and Pakistan. Cordovez eventually negotiated what came to be known as the Geneva Accords. Signed in April 1988, the Accords oversaw a Soviet withdrawal from Afghanistan. Cordovez was nominated for the Nobel Peace Prize for his efforts. Following the signing of the Geneva Accords, a UN body was set up to monitor them. This body was called UNGOMAP—United Nations Good Offices Mission in Afghanistan and Pakistan.

UNGOMAP, in turn, was succeeded by OSGAP—Office of the Secretary-General in Afghanistan and Pakistan. Benon V. Sevan succeeded Cordovez on 15 March 1990. The significance of Benon's full title, from the Soviet Union's standpoint, was that it acknowledged that the war in Afghanistan was an international affair and that Pakistan was deeply involved. The fact that Benon was the secretary-general's "personal representative" showed he was not acting on behalf of the Security Council, but that he was employing the "good offices" of the secretary-general.[3]

Meanwhile, the Afghanistan portfolio, which Benon inherited in 1990, was a deteriorating situation disguised as a challenge. It was a time bomb, inexorably ticking. The Geneva Accords, like the accords to end the Vietnam war negotiated by Henry Kissinger more than a decade earlier to end another superpower failure, created a framework for peace, but that framework was built on a false foundation. The negotiators worked in good faith, but the parties to the Geneva Accords never intended to honor them. They signed with their fingers crossed and their weapons cocked. Benon inherited a disintegrating system of shifting alliances, a centrifugal force without a center.

In the two years since the Accords had been signed, the landscape in and around Afghanistan had changed. For one thing, Cordovez had been authorized to deal only with state governments, not with guerrilla movements within a state. Once the state parties to the Geneva Accords had agreed upon a settlement, however, it became necessary to deal with the warring factions *within* Afghanistan. Although that new option was intended to give the UN more relevance, it had the opposite effect. States are bound by certain international norms, and if they violate those norms, they can be punished—by economic sanctions, by the withdrawal of diplomatic recognition, by expulsion from international bodies, by being denied participation in international treaties, etc. But how does one punish a guerrilla movement, other than by censuring the states that allegedly support its illegal activities?

Further, Zia Ul-Haq, the president of Pakistan, died in a plane crash in 1988, just after the signing of the Geneva

Accords. Cordovez had the distinct impression that Zia could have kept under control the divergent Afghan guerrilla groups in Peshawar. Cordovez also notes ominously that Zia "died in a plane crash, the precise circumstances of which have not, to my knowledge, been fully established."[4]

Thus, Benon had no Zia, no weapon for international censure against guerrilla groups, and not even very much good will. The Pakistan government was still angry that the Accords might allow for a broad-based coalition, which would include communist participation, to serve as an interim government in Afghanistan. They (and their major military backer, the United States, and their major financial backer, Saudi Arabia) wanted no communist participation in an interim government. Pakistan and Saudi Arabia wanted an Islamic state, while the reigning Reagan administration, in part a captive of its own virulent anticommunist policy, wanted total victory over communism, not a coalition, whatever the cost.

In particular, the United States, Pakistan, and Saudi Arabia wanted Najibullah out. That policy had already been recognized in 1988 by Cordovez:

> All my talks with Afghans also led me to conclude that my efforts would be particularly useful if I was able to persuade Najibullah to step down. An intra-Afghan dialogue could start, I had been told, only if all the participants were on an equal footing. If the Soviet withdrawal was the first requirement for the solution of the Afghan conflict, the continuation of a regime set up by the occupying power would be seen by a vast majority of Afghans as an intolerable obstacle. Inasmuch as the resistance leaders and field commanders did not recognize the legitimacy of Najibullah's gov-

ernment, military operations against Kabul and other cities under his control might continue.[5]

Thus, Benon's options were limited, and mined with obstacles. Whereas he was authorized to implement a policy in line with existing accords, he could not, in effect, pursue the implications of those accords. Clearly, there were communists in Afghanistan, and any suggestion in the accords that an Afghan government should represent all the people of Afghanistan, chosen in a manner consistent with their national traditions, meant that Afghan communists had the right to participate in an interim authority—as did mujahidin groups supported by Iran. The UN General Assembly had noted in its resolution 46/23 of 5 December 1991 that there should be in Afghanistan "a broad-based government to ensure the broadest support and immediate participation of all segments of the Afghan people." There were communists in Afghanistan opposed to Najibullah, most significantly, those loyal to Babrak Karmal. To depose Najib would not mean eliminating communism from Afghanistan. Thus, to deny communist representation was contrary to the spirit of the Accords and the resolutions of the UN General Assembly.

The Geneva Accords were noble, thorough, and, in part, fictional. Here, for example, are two paragraphs from the *Bilateral Agreement Between the Republic of Afghanistan and the Islamic Republic of Pakistan on the Principles of Mutual Relations, in Particular on Non-Interference and Non-Intervention*:

Each High Contracting Party undertakes to comply with the following obligations:

(4) to ensure that its territory is not used in any manner with would violate the sovereignty, political

independence, territorial integrity and national unity
or disrupt the political, economic and social stability
of the other High Contracting Party;

(8) to prevent within its territory the training,
equipping, financing and recruitment of mercenaries
from whatever origin for the purpose of hostile activities against the other High Contracting Party, or the
sending of such mercenaries into the territory of the
other High Contracting Party and accordingly to deny
facilities, including financing for the training, equipping and transit of such mercenaries.

The Government of Pakistan never intended to abide
by the Accords it signed in Geneva on 14 April 1988. Barnett Rubin makes clear that the goals of Pakistan's President Zia were not simply to have a "neutral" Afghanistan
but also to have an Afghanistan sympathetic to or under
the control of Pakistan. Rubin corroborates his argument
with reference to an astonishing commentary by then
United States Secretary of State George Shultz in his memoir, *Turmoil and Triumph*:

> Zia had opposed signing the Accords without an
> interim government, but Prime Minister Junejo out-
> maneuvered him by calling a round-table conference
> of all Pakistani political parties. Nearly all parties,
> especially Benazir Bhutto's Pakistan People's Party,
> endorsed signing the agreement even without an
> interim government. This decision led Zia, supported
> by the ISI [Inter-Services Intelligence], to support . . .
> overthrowing Najibullah and installing a mujahideen
> government by military means. According to Shultz,
> when President Reagan asked Zia how Pakistani lead-
> ers would handle their commitment to violate the
> agreement, Zia replied that they would 'just lie about

it. We've been denying our activities there for eight years.' Then, the president recounted, Zia told him that "'Muslims have the right to lie in a good cause.'"[6]

Poor Benon. Poor Afghanistan. To have to deal with liars who sanctify their deceit is the worst nightmare of all for a negotiator. How could Benon convince Najib to resign on the basis of a deal with Pakistani-supported mujahidin when he knew Pakistan was determined to break any agreement that did not give it exclusive power?

The UN's attempt to help Najibullah flee the country he had led brutally for almost five years, and allegedly plundered for many more, raised important issues, not the least of which was to question the extent to which the UN should negotiate with and in this case rescue political leaders widely considered though not legally adjudged to be war criminals.

But to ask this question is to misunderstand the uniqueness of the United Nations as the world's premier international organization. Whereas individual states may refuse to recognize, or negotiate with, official representatives of another state, the UN cannot be that selective. It cannot refuse to speak with the representatives of a member state whose sovereignty it officially recognizes. That is what the principle of universality (having every nation represented at the UN) is all about, and that is one of the reasons member states approach the UN when they cannot speak directly to another state. The General Assembly or the Security Council may set limits on what the secretary-general can discuss, but it cannot credibly ask the secretary-general to avoid contact indefinitely with a member state, even when that state's officials are nonrepresentative, as was the case for many years with "Nationalist" China, with Najibullah until 1992, or with the Northern Alliance from 1996 until the Taliban was overthrown. In each of these three cases, the delegation that held the seat at the UN controlled less than 15 percent of the territory it represented. Moreover, there is nothing in the record to suggest that the secretary-general, through his personal representative, ever discussed matters with Najibullah that the Security Council or the General Assembly had not authorized him to discuss.

As for the UN's attempt to "protect" Najibullah, that was a matter of political, not moral, obligation. All the Afghan players in the war agreed, as Diego Cordovez noted, that "if the Soviet withdrawal was the first requirement for the solution of the Afghan conflict, the continuation of a regime set up by the occupying power would be seen by a vast majority of Afghans as an intolerable obstacle."[7] The secretary-general's decision to press Najib to resign came at the behest of all the major players in the conflict. And in order to convince Najib to resign, the secretary-general had to guarantee Najib's safety. Otherwise, he would in effect be telling Najib, *please put your head in this noose so we can get on with the peace process*. And implicit in guaranteeing Najib's safety was the assumption that the UN would provide him safe departure out of Afghanistan, so that he would not become a potential trophy for his successor. The secretary-general was not in a position to judge Najibullah's guilt or innocence. That was for history, or a properly constituted international tribunal, to judge. The UN's job was to get Najibullah to relinquish power so that the peace process would have a chance to go forward. Peace could not come while Najib was in power. That it did not come after he had resigned was unfortunate. But the effort had to be made.

Meanwhile, Najib's unanticipated request for asylum on UN premises within Afghanistan created several problems. Once the UN had secured Najib's resignation and promised him safe passage, it could not abandon him. To abandon him would have undermined the UN's credibility, not only in Afghanistan but anywhere else in the world where the UN might be called upon to negotiate the resignation of an unpopular leader. At the same time, giving asylum to Najib also affected the UN's credibility by casting it as the sole protector of a hated dictator and by casting doubt on whether the international community would be able to provide security for other leaders, factional or international, who might come to Kabul to negotiate. Najib's failed escape created a lose-lose situation for the UN. More than ever, Najib became an obstacle to peace, the very obstacle the UN had sought to remove. By securing Najib's resignation and then being unable to get him out of the country, the UN had contributed to, even augmented, the creation of a power vacuum in Afghanistan. Like the negotiator who tries to broker the release of hostages and then becomes a hostage himself, the UN was sucked into a power vacuum it had helped to create.

Gianni Picco, who held the Afghanistan portfolio in New York while Benon was in Kabul, recounts his opposition to having the UN take Najib out of the country until there was a secure authority to replace him. He writes that he asked Benon during a conversation, "Who will take power in Kabul [once Najib leaves]?"[8] Picco asserts that Benon had no "fallback position" if he couldn't get Najib out of the country. Benon himself denies this conversation ever took place. But my concern here is not with the veracity of either official; it is with the issue itself. Whether or not it actually happened during a particular telephone conversation, this dialogue took place in the minds of Picco,

Benon, the secretary-general, and everyone else who dealt with the war in Afghanistan. Benon could not have been unaware of this problem. Besides, Benon never intended for this problem to arise. His intention was to bring with him to Kabul from Peshawar, in the UN plane, a council that would take power in Afghanistan, and then to load Najib onto that same plane and leave immediately for New Delhi.

The larger considerations, however, for the sake of historical relevance, are: What is the UN's role in situations where a power vacuum exists? Should it leap into the breach? Should it refuse to intervene in a conflict until it can identify a center of authority, or a few distinct figures with whom it can deal? Can a power vacuum be accurately predicted? And if it can be, is it more or less important than the need to secure the withdrawal of a leader who is an obstacle to peace? The debacle of Najibullah's aborted escape brings these questions to the fore, and while each political situation is unique, there should be a general policy adopted by the international community, a policy that can be modified, depending upon the particular circumstances of the situation, but that should be the norm from which all variations depart.

Defenders of the UN Charter will say that such a norm already exists, namely, that there should be no interference in the internal affairs of a member state. But what of a state like Somalia, which for months before the UN's arrival, did not have, and years later still does not have, a central government? Should the UN stay out of a chaotic domestic situation in which tens of thousands of people are dying of hunger and malnutrition because there is no central authority to invite it to intervene? In fact, the UN's brief stay in Somalia had many successes. When international forces first arrived there in spring 1992—coincidentally, shortly before the collapse of Najibullah's regime in Kabul—there were few children under the age of five alive in Somalia. They had all died from hunger or malnutrition. The UN and international aid agencies reversed that situation. One might even argue that the ultimate failure of UN international forces in Somalia came not from the UN's dubious mandate but from excesses committed by military contingents not under direct UN command, which provoked violent reactions from Somali irregulars. In the three years of its presence in Somalia, the UN even had its military successes, having virtually pacified the entire country with the exception of southern Mogadishu, which was the only area on which the international press seemed to focus.

In any case, there are policymakers within the United States, as well as in Russia, China, and many developing countries (which provide troops for peacekeeping missions) who believe that, with rare exception, the UN should stay out of matters that are largely within the sovereign territory of a member state unless the government of that state invites them in.

My own experience in Afghanistan and in other peace-keeping missions has led me to agree that UN military intervention while a war is still in progress should, with rare exception, be restricted to conflicts between or among states, rather than within a state. For the UN to become entangled in internal strife, in civil wars, in fratricidal conflicts, is a certain recipe for disaster. Moreover, UN forces on such occasions are doomed to become a part of the problem rather than a part of the solution. They become hostages of the "authority" in whose territory they are stationed. Basic operations like resupplying their own troops with food and water may mean having to fight their way through hostile territory, as it did in Bosnia, since local forces are in desperate need of the same basic supplies as are UN troops. Though it may seem callous not to intervene militarily in internecine battles, the alternative may well be a prolongation of the conflict, a loss of credibility, and failure. There are those, understandably, who argue against standing idly by while civil wars rage. And yet, intervention always favors one party to the conflict, and no single party can claim exclusive possession of the moral high ground. To intervene militarily can be just as "immoral," and often more so, if it brings with it false hope. Governments may exert political pressure, press diplomacy, and provide humanitarian aid, but UN military intervention should not become a common occurrence; and when it does occur, the goals of the mission should be clear, the resources should be adequate, and the mandate precise. The loved ones of those brave men and women who return home in body bags deserve no less.

The temptation to intervene militarily becomes particularly strong when there are massive violations of human rights, even when those violations are within the territorial boundaries of a sovereign state. But the fact is, never in history has military intervention been undertaken solely for humanitarian purposes. Military incursions (including NATO's murderous air campaign against Yugoslavia in 1999, allegedly to protect Kosovar Albanians) are taken for strategic, economic, and military purposes, not for humanitarian purposes. Wars are not humanitarian, and the world has not advanced to a new dimension in political thinking simply because the Christian calendar has recently observed the start of a new millennium. Military intervention on the pretext of protecting human rights should not be confused with the ancient goals of imperial domination. Resort to military force is more often a sign of desperation than of determination. Diplomacy should always take precedence.

Of course, diplomacy must be backed by credible military force, and the international community did not have any military force to support its diplomatic efforts in Afghanistan during the period covered in this book. At the same time, the major powers must recognize that very often the conflicting parties within a state that has no dominant leadership (Lebanon, Somalia, Afghanistan) are nothing more than lawless gangs. In such cases, to intervene militarily on one side or the other is merely to choose one's favorite gang. The people of the world, who are paying the bill for such interventions, both in cash and in blood, must not be duped by slick slogans. Governments that divide the warring factions in a civil war into "good guys" and "bad guys" are not only deceiving their own people but are attempting to impose a solution that has no possibility of enduring.

In Bosnia and in Kosovo, for example, NATO has arrogated to itself the responsibility of being the babysitter of the Balkans. That task may well continue for the next half century. But rather than scramble interminably to shore up an unrealistic structure, it would be far better to build a new structure. The Dayton Accords are a failure. Better to recognize realities on the ground and build up from them, rather than seek to impose a foundation from the top. Peace agreements, like architectural structures must be built from the bottom up, not vice versa.

From Tito to Bill Clinton, the world community has had to listen to relentless diatribes against ethnic nationalism. Yet in the Balkans, as in Afghanistan, where tribal loyalties are long and deep, it is time to realize that ethnic nationalism might actually be used positively to bring about a long-term peace. To see nationalism as only destabilizing is to be too rigid. Time and again, voters in the Balkans, in spite of all NATO has done and spent to influence elections, have voted nationalist tickets. Given the opportunity to vote, Afghan citizens would do the same. Perhaps it is time, therefore, to recognize that ethnic nationalism may actually be an intermediate step toward true national sovereignty. Once each ethnic community feels secure within its own region, it will proceed to integrate with other communities and with the nation as a whole though commerce, trade, cultural exchanges, intermarriage, and so forth. As American currency reminds us, *e pluribus unum*. Out of the many, one. The "many" are often ethnic communities. They must be acknowledged as the many before they can join into being one.

Of course the UN cannot refuse a demand by the Security Council to intervene in the domestic matters of a sovereign state, if that demand is made. At the same time, the UN cannot afford to find itself in the position of what in commerce is known as a "receiver." In a sense, countries without a central authority, such as Somalia, or Afghanistan directly after Najib's resignation (or those without an infrastructure and a functioning civil service, such as East Timor following its vote in favor of independence), are countries in receivership. And although there are those in the UN, as in any governmental or intergovernmental organization, who would like to expand the reach of their authority, one should seriously consider limiting the UN's intervention during a conflict to diplomatic and political functions, rather than military. Quite simply, the UN does not have the military capacity to intervene in major conflicts, and never will have, because the big powers will never give it that authority, which might conceivably undermine their own sovereignty. Thus, while the United Nations cannot remain passive in the face of massive violations of human rights within the sovereign territory of a member state, neither can it, with no standing army, expect to impose itself militarily on well-armed and well-financed combatants. In UN terminology, military intervention should be for the purposes of peace*keeping* (postconflict), rather than peace*making*.

Postconflict intervention must have its guidelines. In order for a UN peacekeeping operation to be successful, there must be a kind of political syzygy: an alignment of domestic, international, and global interests. There must be agreement on the terms of peace within the country among the warring parties; outside the country among the front-line states; and at the super power, or global, level. Moreover, there is nothing more demoralizing to United Nations personnel in the field, civilian as well as military, than to have the Security Council give the United Nations a mandate, and then have powerful states immediately begin to undermine that mandate, for purely domestic reasons, as soon as they emerge from the Security Council chamber.

In former Yugoslavia, there was no political syzygy at all. The Serbs, the Croatians, and the Muslims were never in agreement; the United States and Russia were not in agreement, and the United States and Western Europe, although allies, had significant policy differences, particularly regarding the use of force.[9] In Afghanistan following the Soviet Union's withdrawal, the only agreement among industrial democracies was to stay out, thereby allowing Pakistani expansionism to have its way.

Humanitarian assistance is another matter, but that also has ramifications. To begin with, it's a huge business that employs a large number of people and involves the purchase of tremendous assets from multinational corporations, assets then distributed "free" to a target population. (Some assets are donated, but many are purchased.) Both the contributing corporations and the organizations that distribute them have political leverage at every step of the operation, and even have an investment in keeping the aid operation going. I am not suggesting there is any sort of nefarious conspiracy involved here. Most workers in such operations, especially at ground level, are truly idealistic, but there are times when the constant wish to expand operations may benefit corporate contributors more than the indigent recipients. Moreover, the many contracts that are negotiated, from personnel to transportation vehicles to the furniture that adorns the offices of such organizations, involves large amounts of power brokering and money. In short, there is more to "aid" operations than many realize.

Humanitarian aid also has a political dimension in the country where it is distributed, whether Somalia or Afghanistan or Rwanda. It invariably sustains the authority in power. On the other hand, while it is intended to provide vital assistance to those in need, much aid never reaches its target. Instead, it is siphoned off by local militias, thus strengthening their ability to prolong the conflict. The question of distribution, of who gets what and how, is critical. If the international community insists on controlling the distribution of its own aid within a sovereign state, it functions as an occupying power, as an independent government, which is usually outside its mandate and beyond its capability. Yet, if it defers to local authorities, the aid may never reach its target population. During a civil war, there is little security. Aid shipments are frequently looted. Roads are not secure, warehouses are not secure. It is not enough simply to assemble relief supplies, with the noble intention of relieving those in dire need.

Then there is the matter of the profound contradiction between imposing economic sanctions on a country and, at the same time, spending billions of dollars in aid to supply what could well have been locally produced, or traded for, if those sanctions had never been imposed. There is also the danger of using the cover of humanitarian aid operations to promote espionage and subversion.

In Afghanistan during the time I was there, the political structure, such as it was, could not adequately host international aid operations. The humanitarian agencies were conscientious, courageous, and tenacious, but they were constantly frustrated. Political stability, including law and order, is an essential component for efficient humanitarian operations. Unfortunately, the needy can seldom wait for such luxuries when they are cold and hungry. Starving children do not understand politics; and so, humanitarian aid with all its shortcomings continues in many parts of the world, as it did in 1992 in Afghanistan. At the same time, those who plan humanitarian aid cannot pretend they are above politics.

A recent blue-ribbon Panel on United Nations Peace Operations has sought to suggest a direction for future UN peace operations, in the light of lessons learned from several operations during the 1990s—in Somalia, Rwanda, former Yugoslavia, and Sierra Leone, among others. Afghanistan is not mentioned because it was not officially a peacekeeping operation.[10] But I note the report here because it is a critical document and should be considered when discussing any UN peace operation, even in retrospect. Its principles will no doubt be applied to any future peacekeeping operation in Afghanistan. In fact, the chair of the panel that produced the report was Lakhdar Brahimi, the Algerian diplomat who was the UN's chief negotiator in Afghanistan following the terrorist attacks of September 11, 2001. Brahimi was instrumental in organizing the talks that led to the Bonn Agreement of 5 December 2001, and to the establishment of an interim government on 22 December headed by Hamid Karzai.

The panel divided UN peace operations into what it termed three principal activities: "conflict prevention and peacemaking, peacekeeping, and peace-building." The first two categories are largely self-explanatory. Peacemaking involves "building a solid foundation for peace" and addresses conflicts in progress. It relies mainly on diplomacy and mediation. Peacekeeping is concerned with keeping the peace, once there is a peace to keep. In the past, it has involved coming between warring factions and keeping them apart. These two activities have been going on for half a century.

The concept of peace-building, however, which is fairly recent, is likely to be attempted increasingly in the first decade of the twenty-first century. It will be attempted in Afghanistan. The language of the panel's report is at times highly idealistic and at times terrifyingly Orwellian. Perhaps such ambiguity is the stuff of political rhetoric, but in its attempt to justify military intervention by the powerful against the weak, the report at times sounds more like a Holy Crusade than the *raison d'être* of the world's premier international organization. Here is how the panel defines peace-building:

> Peace-building...defines activities undertaken on the far side of conflict to reassemble the foundations of peace and provide the tools for building on those foundations something that is more than just the absence of war. Thus, peace-building includes but is not limited to reintegrating former combatants into civilian society, strengthening the rule of law (for example, through training and restructuring of local police, and judicial and penal reform); improving respect for human rights through the monitoring, education and investigation of past and existing abuses; providing

technical assistance for democratic development (including electoral assistance and support for free media); and promoting conflict resolution and reconciliation techniques.

One shudders at the implications of phrases like "the far side of the conflict" or "support for free media." How far is the far side of the conflict? Does it include monitoring and/or regulating military, social and economic activities, and perhaps the lives of private citizens in a country having been deemed an "aggressor"? In post-Taliban Afghanistan, will it mean tracking suspected Taliban sympathizers for the next few decades? How long do such activities last? Ten years? Fifty years? In perpetuity? Until the international community decides country X can run its own affairs "democratically"—that is, in accordance with the best interests of the major powers? Until Afghanistan has joined the global economy? Even democratic elections do not necessarily qualify a country to govern itself. How many elections has Bosnia had to this date? And does "support for free media," a noble concept, justify acts such as NATO's bombing of Serbian broadcasting studios because they wouldn't stop airing criticism of what they and much of the world considered to be NATO's military aggression against their sovereign country in 1999?

Another portion of the document demeans the time-honored concept of "impartiality" by advising UN field commanders to ignore their mandate when necessary and adhere to the higher values of the United Nations Charter. Here is an excerpt from the panel's executive summary of its section on the need for "robust doctrine and realistic mandates."

Impartiality for United Nations operations must therefore mean adherence to the principles of the

Charter: where one party to a peace agreement clearly and incontrovertibly is violating its terms, continued equal treatment of all parties by the United Nations can in the best case result in ineffectiveness and in the worst may amount to complicity with evil.

How is one to interpret such rhetoric? Does this mean that a carefully crafted mandate should be summarily abandoned (under whose authority?) if it has been decided that adherence to principles of the Charter supersede that mandate? How could a mandate have been adopted in the first place if it contradicted the Charter? By definition, all mandates comply with the Charter. Retribution for violating an agreement should be specified within the agreement, not imposed by appeal to a mystical absolute, in this case the higher authority of the Charter. Such language is simply an attempt to justify the use of force against one of the parties to the conflict. How is one to trust an international organization that enters a sovereign country under the cloak of a specific mandate, a mandate that has been agreed to by all parties to the conflict, and then arbitrarily decides to reinterpret that mandate—in effect, to side with one gang against another gang—*without altering its mandate*? This is what happened in Somalia, and the result was a disaster. What is the point of having a mandate in the first place, if it is to be transcended at some point in accordance with a divine perception of moral rectitude, rather than by a vote in the body that first authorized it?

Or, is the panel saying that political impartiality in the implementation of a mandate is only necessary when there are two superpowers between which one seeks to be impartial? One cannot be impartial between one power. One can only be impartial between two powers, or among several powers. In this sense, the phrase "party to a peace agreement" in the panel's report must be deconstructed, since it is the prevailing superpower that decides when one of the parties to the agreement is violating its terms. *Party to a peace agreement* must be read to mean *super powers that support the peace agreement*. And if this deconstruction seems unfair, then let me give a practical example.

In Bosnia, there were many times when the Bosnian Serbs violated Security Council resolutions, as well as numerous local agreements. There were also times (not as many) when the Muslims and the Croatians violated Security Council resolutions and local agreements. But it was politically impossible to bomb the Muslims or the Croatians. One reason it was impossible was that UN troops in Bosnia were stationed mainly on territory controlled by the Muslims. They would have become hostages and victims. The larger reason was that NATO and CNN had made the determination that the Bosnian Serbs were evil and morally reprehensible and that the other parties to the conflict were victims who could do no evil.

This bias brings up the next loaded phrase: *complicity with evil*. Who decides what is evil? This phrase is too vague unless qualified *within a mandate*. If a mandate adopted by the Security Council says that UN troops are in a country to protect the delivery of humanitarian aid, it takes a great stretch of political imagination for the field commander to decide that he has suddenly recognized the presence of evil and must now attack one of the parties to the conflict. It would be more responsible for him to retaliate against *any* party that interferes with the delivery of humanitarian aid, since that is his mandate.

Moreover, how is the international community to train peacekeeping troops to recognize *complicity with evil*? Should troops be given Evil Awareness Training (EAT) before they are dispatched to the field? Should they carry religious texts with them into battle, rather than small arms? Should they brandish crosses to protect themselves from the vampires of iniquity?

One last point. The panel's report contains many good recommendations, in spite of its occasional excesses and righteous fervor. Among the most important is one that the secretary-general should not deploy troops into the field until he has a full complement of those promised to him. Governments in the past have pledged troops but never delivered them, and sometimes they have delivered them without even the most basic necessities—without proper training, weapons, or even boots. Meanwhile, the United States continues to refuse to pay its full peacekeeping assessments at the same time that it insists on directing peacekeeping operations. Such irresponsibility on the part of the world's only superpower undermines the credibility both of Washington's goals and of UN troops in the field.

Finally, outside intervention into a civil conflict is necessarily selective, and therefore easily mistrusted. The UN is not going to intervene in Spain's conflict with the Basques, nor should it. But imagine Washington telling Madrid that unless it granted autonomy to the Basque people, which had been busily assassinating Spanish police officers, the United States would bomb Madrid. (Substitute *Kosovar Albanians* for Basques, and *Belgrade* for Madrid, and you have the incredible rationalization for NATO's air war against Yugoslavia.) Each situation is unique in international affairs, but a better argument will have to be found for violating national sovereignty than a hypocritical appeal to the UN Charter. Inhumane treatment by a government against its citizens is a lethal illness infecting the body politic. It cannot be allowed to continue, but the remedy for such crimes must not be worse than the illness.

In Afghanistan, there will always be a question as to whether the chaos that followed the UN's unsuccessful attempt to evacuate Najibullah would have taken place anyway. There are those who will say that such chaos was inevitable. But what is certain is that the situation clearly worsened as a result of the incident.

For one thing, Najib himself became an issue. Whereas before only his leadership had been an issue, now his very person became an issue. Who would arrest and possibly try him? Who would claim jurisdiction over his fate? Who would be responsible for his life?

The UN's premises, as well as its credibility, also became issues. They were no longer merely the headquarters of an international observation mission; they were now the safe haven for a hated dictator. Would UN premises be stormed? Would its local employees be harassed?

If Najib had been evacuated successfully, none of those issues would have arisen. And the sudden injection of additional issues at a time when ongoing negotiations were already precarious had the effect of distracting the actors. It clouded their focus. Najib's fate became more of a concern than the membership of the Council of Impartials.

There was also the matter of the UN's credibility as an impartial broker. How could the UN now avoid the accusation that it favored Najib, that it had made a secret deal with him? Impartiality, no matter how much that concept is derided by those who favor the use of force in international relations, is an essential component of any peacekeeping operation. And in the eyes of many, most importantly the conflicting parties themselves, the UN had compromised its impartiality by trying to evacuate Najib surreptitiously.

If Najib's escape had taken place as planned, the intensity of criticism against the UN would have been less. The debate would have been more academic than sanguinary, and Najib's personal fate would have been less of a priority. But failure had begot failure.

The incentive to attack Kabul increased so long as Najib remained in the city, even more so after he had resigned and was holed up like a trapped animal. The race to seize Najib, the crown jewel of communist brutality, was almost a reason in itself for attacking Kabul. Najib's head became a prize.

As for Benon Sevan, he was also a victim, betrayed by forces beyond his control. The question of whether he should ever have been put in the situation of having had to make the decision he made begs the issue. The alternative—by the spring of 1992, when I arrived in Kabul—would have been for the UN to withdraw from Afghanistan, and not return until the situation stabilized itself. That course of action, however, ignores among other things how close Benon was to arriving at an agreement on the composition of a council intended to take power after Najib resigned. Negotiations were close to succeeding. They fell apart only at the last minute when two of the seven mujahidin groups meeting in Peshawar refused to go along with a proposed slate that included nationalist representatives. They wanted a completely Islamic government. And while the argument continued in Peshawar, an ambitious field commander inside Afghanistan seized Kabul's airport, blocked Najib's escape, and initiated a new reign of destruction.

––––––––

The tragedy of Afghanistan during the last two decades of the twentieth century was one of geopolitics, not of genes, even though respected commentators are fond of talking about the "wild tribes" that roamed through the forbidding mountains of this spectacularly beautiful land, and how difficult it had always been to unify them. There has, indeed, been ethnic conflict in Afghanistan, and it still persists. But the critical component, the ultimate catalyst, that set off the Soviet Union's invasion of Afghanistan in 1979, was rooted in geopolitics. If Afghanistan had not been positioned between the Soviet Union's oil-rich southern flank and Iran and the Persian Gulf, as well as within striking distance of China, its fate would have been much less turbulent. What spurred the decaying and increasingly myopic Soviet leadership to think it had to invade Afghanistan was not the wish to have an outlet to the warm waters of the Persian Gulf. It was the fear that Afghanistan might become "neutral"—that it might become an Asian Yugoslavia.

As Cordovez and Harrison remark:

> Moscow did not launch its invasion as the first step in a master plan to dominate the Persian Gulf, as most observers believed at the time. Rather, after stumbling into a morass of Afghan political factionalism, the Soviet Union resorted to military force in a last desperate effort to forestall what it perceived as the threat of an American-supported Afghan Tito on its borders.[11]

Nationalist rivalries are, for the most part, an internal affair. But since nations, by definition, have borders, their internal developments inevitably have consequences for their neighbors. In Afghanistan's case, the analogy to former Yugoslavia was particularly appropriate. Neutrality is the flip side of nationalism. Nations caught between the ambitions of powerful rivals often feel their very survival depends on maintaining a national identity, so as not to goad either rival into annexing them. To have your own identity as a small nation is to be neutral in the rivalry between great powers. Tito's success in Yugoslavia was not because he had a tough hand; Balkan leaders have always had a tough hand. It was because he maintained a balance between the two superpowers and was able to get economic infusions from both camps. The fact that he was one of the founders of the Non Aligned Movement gave great support to his neutrality. Afghanistan had no such political magician.

Though there was a divergence of opinion in the Soviet Union about whether or not to invade Afghanistan, once the deed was done, it became difficult to reverse course. Selig Harrison, in fact, makes a trenchant comment on the connection between the national intrigue inside Afghanistan and the self-consuming paranoia within the Soviet Union.

> The story behind the invasion begins in Kabul with a Byzantine sequence of murderous Afghan intrigue, complicated by turf wars between rival Soviet intelligence agencies and the undercover manipulations of agents for seven contending foreign powers. It reaches its climax when Brezhnev, ailing and alcoholic, pushes through the decision to invade in secrecy without calling a full meeting of his Politburo, disregarding the opposition of three key generals in his Army General Staff.[12]

Another major factor in Afghanistan's civil war during the 1990s was narcotics. Regrettably, the poppy plant was a greater motivation than the Koran for contending armies inside Afghanistan. In 1999, after the Taliban (bred in Pakistan and financed by the United States and Saudi Arabia) had pacified (i.e., brutalized) 85 percent of Afghanistan and imposed Islamic law, which forbids the use of narcotics, the UN Office for Drug Control and Crime Prevention in Vienna reported that Afghanistan had more than doubled its production of opium in the past year, "and now accounts for three-quarters of the world opium crop."[13]

The size of the opium crop in Afghanistan over the next two years went up and down. For the most part it was cultivated in areas under the control of the Taliban, but the Northern Alliance also encouraged poppy growth. At one point in early 2001, the Taliban sharply curtailed its production of opium, but their motives were never clear, and they apparently never reduced their stockpiles. A dispatch filed by *New York Times* correspondent Barry Bearak on 24 May 2001 is filled with praise for the mendacious mullahs of Kandahar: "American narcotics officials who visited the country confirmed earlier United Nations reports that the Taliban had, in one growing season, managed a rare triumph in the long and losing war on drugs. And they did it without the usual multimillion dollar aid packages that finance police raids, aerial surveillance and crop subsidies for farmers."[14]

On 26 September 2001, just fifteen days after the terrorist attack on the World Trade Center, the *Times* reported once again on the Taliban's wonderful work, but this time with a bit more skepticism. Michael R. Gordon and Eric Schmitt wrote that although a UN panel visiting the area in spring 2000 had concluded that poppy cultivation in Afghanistan had been "largely eradicated," the UN also noted that production in the first part of 2000 had increased substantially from the previous year before the ban took effect. In the view of the *Times* reporters, this incongruity raised "the question of whether the Taliban was stocking up."[15]

Ironically, Bearak's story was probably correct in asserting that poppy eradication in Taliban areas occurred without crop subsidies for the farmers, since the Taliban most likely received payouts to curtail production from the World Food Program and humanitarian NGOs (to whom the Bush administration made a $43 million contribution), kept the money for themselves, and spent it on weapons. In other words, the mullahs were subsidized, the farmers were not.

Moreover, it must be assumed that those who can impose a policy with such dramatic efficiency, however laudable that policy might be, can just as easily reverse themselves—especially if the price of opium should rise. It is not unheard of for a producer to withhold production of a commodity in order to drive up its price. Thus, the Taliban most likely received international largesse at the same time that its extensive stocks of opium were increasing in price. Good capitalist tactics.

In any case, it is virtually certain that opium production will resume on a serious basis in post-Taliban Afghan istan, no matter who is in charge. After all, it a major source of revenue for farmers and tax officials. Tim Weiner in the 26 November 2001 edition of the *New York Times*, relates an interview with a poor Afghan farmer who is looking forward to cultivating poppies once again now that that the Taliban has been overthrown. "There is no other way to survive," he tells Weiner. "I have 10 children. There are 28 people in my house."[16] The *Times* estimates that farmers can earn at least one hundred times more from selling opium that from selling vegetables and fruits. Of course. Would we expect McDonald's to abandon fast food in order to sell granola just because the government has changed hands?

2

The

Journal:

April 1992

1 April 1992

In the morning I meet with Giandomenico Picco, assistant secretary-general in the office of Secretary-General Boutros Boutros-Ghali, for a briefing on Afghanistan. The war there continues. It has been going on for more than twelve years. The antagonists change and realign, but the devastation continues. The pain goes on. And there is growing concern that the civil war in Afghanistan may spill over into neighboring Muslim republics and destabilize all of central Asia.

In the coming days, Picco tells me, we will have to determine whether or not the great ethnic divide that had surfaced in the past two weeks will persist. An army led by General Abdul Rashid Dostom [composed largely of Uzbeks], and an army led by General Ahmad Shah Massoud [composed largely of Tajiks], have joined forces. They are in control of most of the northern part of Afghanistan. Will they try to split Afghanistan in two? Will there be a northern and southern Afghanistan?

[Massoud is the most charismatic, the best strategist, and the most politically astute of all the guerilla commanders. When he occupies a village, he sets up a viable administration, provides benefits for the indigent, and restores social services. At the same time, he is a devout Muslim himself, and his wife wears the veil. The Uzbeks, for their part, are legendary for their fierce bravery. Massoud is a trained engineer. Dostom has only a grammar school education.]

The ethnic divide among Afghanistan's population is approximately like this: Pashtun, 38 percent; Tajik, 25 percent; Hazara, 19 percent; Turkmen, up to 10 percent; and Uzbek, 8 percent. The two official languages are Dari (Afghan Persian) and Pashto. The Tajiks, Uzbeks, and Hazara draw support from Iran to the west, as well as from Tajikistan and Uzbekistan, which border Afghanistan to the north. The Pashtun, located largely in eastern and southeastern Afghanistan, around Kabul and Kandahar, respectively, are supported by the large Pashtun population across the border in western Pakistan, as well as by the governments of Pakistan and Saudi Arabia. But in fact, there are so many conflicting allegiances among ethnic groups in the region that any alliance or simple explanation seems doomed to dissipate, which is one reason that some favor the return of the exiled King as a figure who might bring the various factions together.

There is another factor too. There is an urban-rural dichotomy in Afghanistan, the same problem that plagues virtually all developing countries, and even some industrialized countries. Most of the educated, cultured, professional class that existed in Afghanistan before the last cycle of wars resided in the cities. It was not a large group, but it was almost exclusively urban. The countryside, by contrast, was virtually devoid of talent, except for the occasional government official dispatched to work on a road, a bridge, a dam, or some such project. There are vast areas between cities, throughout the country, that are effectively controlled by bandits. The village people often distrust, and consider immoral, their urban counterparts. The urban professionals, meanwhile, may have a sentimental attachment to the traditions of the countryside, but choose not to live there. They prefer plumbing and electricity to folk customs when push comes to Pashto.

[James Michener, in his novel *Caravans*, makes the following comment, which is as appropriate today as it was when he made it in 1963: "The future history of Afghanistan, if left to Afghans, would be determined by the struggle between the many bearded mullahs from the hills and the few young experts . . . with degrees from Oxford or the Sorbonne or the Massachusetts Institute of Technology."

Michener's phrase "if left to Afghans," reflects his awareness of the continuous and predatory demands on Afghanistan by its neighbors. As for "the many bearded mullahs from the hills," Michener was suggesting that "religious" contention within the world of Islam, at least in Afghanistan, is not as much between the so-called moderate and extreme branches as it is between the urban practitioners who are willing to adapt their faith to the social and scientific advances of civilization and the rural, antiscientific, illogical tyrants who fear losing power.]

The UN, Pico continues, is trying to arrange a meeting of various Afghan leaders that will choose an interim government to take power after President Najibullah leaves office, and until general elections can be held. Najib has already announced that he will resign, although he has not set a specific date. The meeting of Afghan leaders, known as a Loya Jirga, or grand council, would take place at the end of April, probably in Vienna. It cannot take place in

Kabul, because Massoud will not meet there. He feels Tajiks are treated as second-class citizens in Kabul, which is dominated by the Pashtuns. In the period between Najib's resignation and the designation by Afghan leaders of an interim government, there would be a transitional, or pre-interim, council that would assume authority.

The Loya Jirga cannot be held in neighboring Pakistan, because that would make it appear that Pakistan is manipulating the situation [which it is, since it is already supporting several of the mujahidin factions with weapons and recruits]. There has to be a neutral venue. Now that Najibullah has agreed to resign, there must be a credible authority to replace him, and that authority must be identified quickly in order to avoid a power vacuum. [Picco is very concerned about a power vacuum. It is his major concern.]

Both Iran and Pakistan have said they would support the UN initiative to convene a Loya Jirga. They have particular interest in stabilizing the situation in Afghanistan, because they cannot absorb more refugees. In 1992, Picco says, there were more than 5 million Afghan refugees in their two countries—3 million in Pakistan, and 2 million in Iran.

[In fact, the secretary-general's report of 27 November 1992 states: "The extent of human suffering in Afghanistan has been horrendous: more than 1 million dead, an estimated 2 million disabled, tens of thousands of orphans and widows, over 5 million refugees, and more than 2 million internally displaced persons." The estimated population of Afghanistan in 1992 was between 24 and 25 million, which would mean that at least 20 percent of its population was refugees. If one adds the displaced persons—those that have fled their homes but not their country—the total climbs to almost 30 percent of the population. Afghanis are already the largest refugee population in the world, much larger than the Palestinians, for example, who receive more international assistance and more recognition.]

Political representatives of seven opposition guerrilla movements are currently meeting in Peshawar, Pakistan, under the combined auspices of the UN and Pakistan. Najib, being a Pashtun, would prefer the Loya Jirga to meet in Kabul, Picco notes, but it is not possible, because Najib would be accused of controlling the assembly.

I ask if there would be security problems if the meeting were held in Vienna, and problems with transporting the leaders there.

That is something to discuss with Benon, Picco replies. Yes, there would be problems, but time is short, and we must move before Kabul becomes a battleground. He reiterates his concern about a power vacuum when Najib leaves. Though a few rockets have fallen in Kabul, the city so far has been largely untouched by the war, except for swarms of refugees.

Picco tells me, incidentally, that the Tajiks also have a French connection, in addition to their Iranian supporters. Massoud studied at the French *Lycée* in Kabul and speaks French, which endears him to Paris.

[French influence in the region is negligible at this point, however. Having been blown out of the Persian Gulf by the recent war there, which established American dominance, the French are now seeking to reestablish their links with Islam. Economic embargoes against Iraq eclipsed French long-term contracts with Iraq to be supplied with oil, in payment for goods and technology France had already delivered. France also lost its ability to supply weapons technology to Arab states, who will now buy from the United States. The French also received very little in the way of contracts to rebuild Kuwait. Add to those developments that Iran resents the French for having supported Iraq during the Gulf War, and for having given asylum to Iranian dissidents like Bani Sadr, and France was a big loser in the Gulf War. This disgrace, translated into French francs, has encouraged the French to be mischievous in central Asia in order to regain influence, but they are not a major player.]

Najib gets his main financial support from the sale of natural gas and from trade with Pakistan, whom he considers to be a main antagonist, Picco continues. Business knows no enemies. Meanwhile, Pakistan receives heavy support from Saudi Arabia. "This is a proxy war," Picco tells me. "It is Saudi Arabia [through Pakistan] vs. Iran. The Saudis and the Iranians hate each other. They are bitter rivals, and have transported their rivalry here." Although they are different sects of Islam [the Saudis are Wahabi, and the Iranians are Shi'a], this is not a religious war. It is a war for influence and power. Once the war in Afghanistan is settled, Picco speculates, the battle scene may shift to the former Soviet Muslim republics.

Picco feels that King Zahir Shah may be the best hope for unity, but since the King doesn't want to lead a government, the best choice at this point would be for the Loya Jirga to choose an interim government until elections can eventually be held.

[M. Hassan Kakar, an Afghan historian, asserts that the alliance between Dostom, Massoud, and others, was not intended to split Afghanistan between north and south. On the contrary, he argues, it was intended to take over all of Afghanistan, albeit somewhat naively, since it had no Pashtun representation. Here is Kakar's view of the situation, uncorroborated but credible:

When the Coalition of the North (CN) was established is unknown, but it became active in March 1992 in

Mazar after Abdur Rashid Dostom...rebelled. He did so because Kabul could no longer grant him money and weapons. President Najibullah dispatched a force by air under General Mohammad Nabi Azimi, deputy minister of defense, to silence the rebellion, but Azimi secretly joined Dostom instead. More serious, on 22 March, Ahmad Shah Massoud, Dostom, Azad Beg Kahn, Abduli Ali Mazari and Azimi decided in a meeting to overthrow President Najibullah and set up a new government . . . But the CN was made under ethnic impulse, as none among those who devised it spoke Pashto.[1]]

---

5 April 1992

London. Stopover here on the way to Islamabad. This afternoon I visited Speaker's Corner in Hyde Park, one of my favorite sights in London. I visit it whenever I pass through. It is the epitome of free speech: the right to say anything one wants to [except to threaten to life of the Queen], and to be protected by the police. A great institution.

This time the speakers were mostly religious: Christian and Muslim. There was only one political speaker, a young man looking like Trotsky, espousing socialism. But for the most part I heard no political debate among the population, and I wondered why. Had the end of the Cold War killed political dissent? Had everyone now accepted the inevitability of the global economy? Now that the Soviet empire had fallen, as much from internal corruption and inefficiency as anything else, was there no viable alternative to consumerism and market-oriented greed? Was religious revival, that desperate, deceitful plea to the sick spirit, now emerging as the sole opposition to the ravages of materialism? Perhaps the new dialectic would be between the spiritual and the material, rather than between communism and capitalism.

Or perhaps, as in Afghanistan, spiritual slogans were only concealing material goals. An Iranian friend of mine in the United Nations once told me what the Iranians say about their mullahs. *Beneath the beard, it says: "Made in America."* Most of the high officials in the Iranian government went to universities and business schools in America. They were not fighting for the life of the spirit. They were fighting for control of Iran's huge oil deposits. I also recalled the comments of an Irish friend when I asked him about religious conflict in Northern Ireland. "Religion is only a jersey. Property is the issue," he said.

And I thought about nationalism, which had succeeded Marxism in so many countries. Its dangers were abundantly clear, especially for ethnic minorities within newly independent, developing countries. On the other hand, nationalism was perhaps the most effective ideology for resisting the encroachments of the soul-devouring global economy. There was a certain romanticism, even in Afghanistan, in resisting the predatory octopus of consumerism, which threatened to efface national traditions [even if they were not always humane], and replace them with the sodden, empty sameness of upscale boutiques and fast-food franchises.

There were conflicting attitudes toward Western culture among Afghans as well. Educated technicians and professionals wanted to join the West, while others bitterly opposed what they saw as its corrupt values. For the latter, Western society was prostitution, drugs, Hollywood films, rock music, blue jeans, etc. Massoud, for example, an engineer and a member of the professional class, supported education for all [including women], at the same time that he was a religious fundamentalist. He saw no contradiction there. Not so with Hekmatyar [Pakistan's front man], who was puritanical and regressive, and savagely opposed all Western values.

———————

I have sent postcards to my children. They think I'm crazy to go to Afghanistan in the middle of a war. Too dangerous. Perhaps they're right. Yet, I cannot imagine myself a potential casualty of war at this point. I cannot think about my own mortality. And it is not that I refuse to do so; it is that I don't know where to start. Death is too abstract for me at this time, in this place. Where does one start? Imagining *how* one dies? *Where* one dies? How loved ones will mourn? That is not realism; that is narcissism, a morass of self-pity. Nor can I begin to think about what I would do in a particular situation if my life were threatened. One can never anticipate how he would react in a crisis. No, the best I can do at this point is to think about thinking about death. Or perhaps to contemplate my motivation for having come here, for having volunteered to place myself in harm's way. And in that light I recall those magnificent lines by Yeats in his poem about the Irish airman who foresees his death: "A lonely impulse of delight / Drove to this tumult in the clouds." Though I am not an Irish pilot, nor was meant to be, I can, I do, feel *delight*, the delight of adventure, the naïve electricity of being an agent of peace. Yes, it is true. At the same time, to pose the question of why I came to Afghanistan is to demean the impulse. Why must action [or thought, for that matter] be explained, understood? Only Beckett, that grand cartographer of the absurd, could answer such a question. What is it Molloy says? "One is what one is, partly at least."

───────

8 April 1992

Islamabad. I am sleeping at a place called Canada House. It is owned by the Canadian government. I am in a room that is usually occupied by a colonel who is on leave for two weeks. I will be here only for a day or two, until I can go to Kabul.

My room has a high ceiling and a marble floor. There are several closets. There is a servant for the entire house, a young man in his twenties named Wassim, who is quite pleasant and efficient. He cooks, cleans, presses our suits, attends to our needs. Last night he cooked a meat lasagna; tonight we shall have chili. For breakfast there is cereal, eggs, bread, and tea. I give him 300 rupees (about $12) for three and a half days of food. At the end of my stay I'll give him another 750 rupees (about $30).

My day began at 4:30 a.m., when I was awakened by the birds. They were chattering, crying, complaining. Very loud, just at the hour when rosy-fingered dawn was brightening the sky, and the muezzin was calling the faithful to prayer.

One's first impressions of a country are often abiding, even if not always representative, and my early thoughts of Pakistan were influenced by the behavior of a taxi driver who took me to downtown Islamabad yesterday. He asked me, with natural curiosity, what country I was from. When I told him, he said he liked America. He then volunteered his opinion for the future of the world. He was optimistic, he said, because now after the fall of communism, more people all over the world were able to pray, and he believed that with more prayers God would be more responsive to the needs of people.

I was very touched by his gentle optimism. Though it is

easy to be cynical about such unprovoked professions of
faith, I was very much taken by his sincerity, and the fact
that he included me and my country in his wishes for pros-
perity and good tidings. In fact, I saw his words as much a
form of hospitality as religious expression, although for
many Muslims there is absolutely no distinction. The
belief in doing good works calls upon every Muslim to be
hospitable. But I thought of his words in terms of hospitality, because once again I realized how much of a national
asset hospitality is in most developing countries. When
people are indigent and cannot afford to take you boutique-
hopping or buy you tickets to the latest extravaganza, they
can offer you hospitality. And what greater hospitality can
one offer than to pray for your personal welfare, as well as
that of your family and your country?

I also thought of the great divide between the Pakistani
people, the humble and sentimental farmers and shop-
keepers, and their corrupt political leaders.

———

I am reading about Afghanistan, everything I can
get my hands on. Histories, UN documents, press releases.
Everything. And I constantly try to engage people in conversation, especially Pakistanis. I am aware of the long-
simmering hostility between Pakistan and Afghanistan.
Such enmity is not unusual between neighbors, particularly
when those neighbors have been victimized by colonialism,
when boundaries have been fixed by colonial empires on
the basis of where their armies stopped, rather than according to any reasonable geographical or ethnic dividing line.
In the case of Afghanistan, the current dispute goes back to
1893, when King Amir Abdur Rahman Khan of Afghanistan
signed an agreement with Sir Mortimer Durand, who represented the British colonial administration in India. The

agreement created a boundary between Afghanistan and what was eventually to become Pakistan after the division of India. Pakistan maintained that the boundary continued to exist. Afghanistan nationalists consistently discredited the agreement, saying it was not legally binding because it had been signed under duress. Who was Great Britain to decide on what belonged to Afghanistan, they asked. Harrison and Cordovez sum up the controversy this way:

> The Durand Line . . . defined the de facto limits of Afghan territory. Later these conquered areas were handed over to Pakistan when it was created in 1947. [Mohammed] Daoud [who overthrew Afghanistan's former King Zahir Shah in 1973] had long spearheaded Afghan irredentist demands for an independent, Afghan-linked "Pushtunistan" and a more ambiguously defined Baluch state linking Baluch areas in Pakistan and Iran with a small strip of adjacent Baluch territory in Afghanistan.[2]

> [In August 1999, when I called up information about Afghanistan on the World Wide Web, there was an entry under Afghanistan entitled "Pashtoonistan: The Other Land of Afghans." Ethnic rivalries and territorial claims die slow. Pakistan had reason to be suspicious of Afghan nationalism. In general, multiethnic societies at this point in time are only a slogan in the mouths of neocolonialists who fear for the future of the global economy should tribalism and nationalism join in a common front against them.]

Meanwhile, the UN's limited goal in Afghanistan at this point is to set up as soon as possible a pre-interim Council of Impartials composed of fifteen to twenty souls who will assume authority in Kabul and replace Najibullah, while we prepare for a Loya Jirga. But time is running out. Anarchy seems imminent.

Indeed, the more I read and listen and think, the more I am driven to fear for the near hopelessness of Benon's task. He is Sisyphus rolling the rock of peace up the mountainous terrain of Afghanistan. And the mountains are mined. He is playing the Great Game with a hand of cards dealt by a dubious dealer. He did not choose the game, the hand, or the stakes. In fact, we are all players in a poker game with numerous wild cards, except that we do not know how many or which cards they are. The chips are human lives. The pot is Kabul. Benon is neither impresario nor dealer.

My adrenaline is pumping. I have begun to feel anxious.

———

Last night at Canada House I listened to a British woman who was returning home to England after having served many months in Kabul as a nurse with the ICRC (International Committee of the Red Cross). She was with her boyfriend, a Polish officer, who had also been serving in Kabul and was on his way back to Poland. She had deep blue eyes and blonde hair, and was a bit plump. He was tall and dark and had a mustache. They were in their thirties. They wanted to visit Lahore before leaving Pakistan, but it was difficult to book a flight. The flights to Lahore from Islamabad were infrequent, and always filled. The best way to get a seat was to show up early at the airport and wait for a vacancy. But that meant rising very early in the morning, at 4 or 5 a.m., driving a couple of hours, and perhaps *not* being able to get a seat.

[Neither of them wanted to speak about Kabul, Afghanistan, the UN, or anything political. But it was not as if they had been told to avoid political discussion. It was simply that they didn't care about politics. And I couldn't blame them. I suspected they had done their respective jobs well enough, and now they were finished with Afghanistan. Perhaps they had even done better than they would have if they had been involved in Afghan politics. They just wanted to have fun. On the other hand, I myself was so hungry for discussion and information about Afghanistan, I could scarcely contain my enthusiasm.]

Benon is in town, and when Benon is in town every day is a working day. He comes to pick me up. It is a very warm day, but Benon insists that we wear jackets and ties. He is going to brief the U.S. ambassador to Pakistan, Nicholas Platt, and he wants me to meet Platt. [I wonder if Platt is a descendant of the Senator Platt who was credited with having formulated the series of noxious provisions that constituted the Platt Amendment and made Cuba a virtual colony of the United States during Teddy Roosevelt's administration.]

We drive through Islamabad. It is a quiet city. There is a residential area that seems, as in most capital cities, completely artificial. It is where diplomats and retired military officers live. Benon's driver takes us past the major landmarks, and soon we are in the quarter where the foreign embassies are located. I can hardly imagine that only days ago I was in imperial New York, and that days from now I will be in war-torn Afghanistan.

Platt is a proper diplomat. He is relaxed, gracious, elegant, knowledgeable. He has the demeanor of a man who has just walked off the eighteenth hole at an exclusive country club. He is carefully controlled and thoroughly unspontaneous.

[In February 1979, the U.S. ambassador in Afghanistan, Adolph Dubs, was murdered. He had been taken hostage by a radical Tajik separatist group called the Oppressed Nation Movement. The group demanded the release of their imprisoned leader by the Afghan government as the price for freeing Dubs. The Afghan government refused to negotiate, contrary to the wishes of the United States. Eventually, Afghan police stormed the hotel room where Dubs was being held. Dubs and two of his kidnappers were killed. The United States has not appointed an ambassador to Afghanistan since then.]

The fact that Platt, as Washington's point man for Afghanistan, is stationed in Islamabad says something about Washington's policies and its limited options. Pakistan is only one of landlocked Afghanistan's several neighbors, but it would hardly be possible for the United States to monitor and intervene in the war from the territory of any other contiguous state: Iran to the west, or Turkmenistan, Uzbekistan, and Tajikistan to the north. Only Pakistan to the east and south is a good friend of the United States. And the United States pays dearly for that friendship. Weapons, food, and any other commodity that it wishes to send to the mujahidin resistance in Afghanistan must be funneled through Pakistan, and much of it is siphoned off by Pakistan for its own use, perhaps as much as 30 percent. What is distributed among the various mujahidin groups in Afghanistan is done in accordance with Pakistan's agenda. In effect, U.S. policy in central Asia is landlocked. It has only one conduit, and that conduit is corrupt, indisputably corrupt.

[Here is Cordovez's take on Pakistani corruption:

> The ISI devised a system for the distribution of US weaponry calculated to strengthen the power of its fundamentalist allies. Instead of dealing directly with the local commanders, as the CIA urged, [Brigadier

General Mohammad] Yousaf [of Pakistan's Foreign Ministry> turned over the arms to the seven resistance leaders, who then allocated the aid to the commanders of their choice. Local commanders had to join one of the parties in order to get weapons. Thus, 67 to 73 percent of the weapons went to fundamentalist parties....The ISI distribution system contributed to the perverse corruption and smuggling in the aid pipeline, including narcotics trafficking on a colossal scale.[3]]

Benon explains to Platt the latest developments in his attempt to organize a Council of Impartials. He also tells Platt of the growing humanitarian crisis in Afghanistan. Platt asks how the United States can support international humanitarian efforts. "Just tell us how we can help," he says. Platt notes that in accordance with a previous request by Benon, Platt had asked Washington to send food to Kabul, where refugee concentrations were growing. Within two days of that request, Washington had announced it would send ten thousand tons of wheat to Kabul. This response, Platt adds, is evidence of United States willingness to cooperate with the UN.

[That wheat never arrived in Kabul. A few Pakistani planes carrying food were shot at while trying to land in Kabul, and Pakistan immediately halted further flights there. Meanwhile, a truck convoy out of Peshawar with food intended for Kabul, when faced with possible hijacking, sabotage, and theft along the long overland route, barely crossed the border into Afghanistan before turning back, according to a reliable United Nations Development Program (UNDP) source in Kabul. A few threats, in other words, and the convoy returned to base. The same UNDP source reported that other food supplies recently arrived in Kabul had been so contaminated that they were useless. During a war, food is a strategic asset. Thus, it had to be expected that mujahidin fighters who controlled the access roads to Kabul would commandeer as much food as necessary to feed their forces, and perhaps the population of those they were trying to enlist in their cause, before allowing any food convoy to pass through to distant Kabul and the hated central government. Moreover, sending the wheat directly to Kabul without distributing portions in outlying provinces only encouraged further immigration into the city, whose population had already swelled from 500,000 to over 2 million as a result of the war. In short, the idea to donate food may have been well intentioned, and may have been good for public relations, but it lacked practical planning, and had been poorly executed. Platt had to know the results of his efforts. He was not a stupid man. He was well informed. On the other hand, he was caught in a bind. If the United States didn't offer to help, it would be criticized as having a depraved indifference to human suffering. If it did offer aid, that aid would never reach its intended target. Faced with such choices, the main strategy was to manipulate information: to publicize the intent to help, but bury the results.]

Platt then informs Benon of what contact he has had with mujahidin political leaders. He says that Burhanuddin Rabbani [a Tajik political leader who represents the interests of General Massoud] has his own list of potential members for the Council of Impartials. He wants his list integrated with Benon's list. Rabbani also has additional demands before he will agree to forming a Council of Impartials. He wants current police organizations disbanded. Secret police, as well as regular police. And he wants to limit the power that any pre-interim Council would have. He estimates that the Council would have to last for at least forty-five days.

[This was the first time I had heard about Rabbani's demands, and I thought they were unrealistic, even if they were only meant as a negotiating position that was subject to compromise. You couldn't possibly have civil order if you disbanded the police force—even if the police were Najib's agents. And you couldn't submit new lists at the last moment. One or two names perhaps, but not an entire new list. And if Rabbani's demands were impractical, then it was likely that the demands of some of the other six mujahidin groups meeting in Pakistan, not to mention the eight that were meeting in Teheran, were also impractical. Impractical demands are a tactic, of course, to make it appear one is negotiating when one has no intention of negotiating. It is far more ambiguous and better for public relations to offer unrealistic proposals than to refuse to negotiate. Meanwhile, the United States and Pakistan didn't want any communists on the Council—which was also unrealistic.]

Benon tells Platt that he thinks the Loya Jirga should be held in Vienna. He repeats, as he has before, that if the meeting is held in Pakistan, Pakistan will be accused of manipulating the results. In the view of Iran, if the meeting is convened in Pakistan, Pakistan will never allow it to proceed. The Pakistanis will disrupt it, because they won't permit any meeting they cannot completely control. And if the meeting is held in Kabul, Najibullah will be accused of manipulating the results. Vienna is a neutral venue.

[There was, in fact, some basis for suspicions that Pakistan might disrupt what would attempt to be an impartial assembly. Cordovez recounts what had happened in February 1989, when a similar meeting was convened:

A broad-based consultative council (*shura*)...was finally convened on February 10, in a huge Muslim pilgrim transit center built by the Government of Pakistan between Islamabad and Rawalpindi. The meeting was preceded by a demonstration in Peshawar on February 8, at which at least seven thousand Afghans protested against the resistance leaders and the "undemocratic" selection of *shura* members...

There was apparently considerable disorder and confusion [once the shura convened, following boycotts by several groups at the last minute]. Mariana Baabar reported in *The Nation* of February 11, that "the chaos and pandemonium resulted in glass doors being smashed, and as stony-faced delegates sat in front of a stage with the seven Peshawar-based leaders, the media were asked to take a quick round of the conference place, and [were] pushed out quickly again." Those who had considered that the *shura* was essentially a manipulation by Pakistan's intelligence services as an alternative, rather than as a first step, to negotiations probably felt that they had been proved right.[4]]

"Najibullah wants one thousand UN troops in Kabul during the transition," Benon continues. "But that is unlikely. Who will pay for them? How can they be recruited in such a short time? We must not be distracted by impossible demands. The meeting in Vienna must be as soon as possible. By the end of the month, at the latest. I hope the UN secretary-general will attend. It will give the meeting added prestige, and emphasize the support of the international community."

[Though Benon is too much of a diplomat to say so, I know that he is concerned about extreme fundamentalist elements, both among the exile mujahidin groups and within the Pakistan government. They are intractable. On the other hand, it is hard to know Platt's opinion. He will never criticize Pakistan, though he is well aware that Pakistan has its own agenda. I think once again at this point about how flawed is the theory that big powers control their clients. The United States cannot control Pakistan's ambition to control Afghanistan; and because it cannot, it has avoided stating any political goals. Instead, it has expressed its wishes for stability in the region as its main goal. But nature, as the saying goes, abhors a vacuum, a political vacuum as well as a physical vacuum, and the absence of a policy is in itself a policy, since it cedes authority to the most powerful player. Nor was I of the opinion that the United States had a secret agenda in Afghanistan that it would not make public. Those familiar with the ineptitude of American foreign policy know well that in many cases there is no policy rather than a clandestine policy. Afghanistan in 1992 was such a case.]

Benon continues to outline his plans. The UN secretary-general will soon be coming to the region. Benon intends to tell the SG what has been accomplished in the past few months, since the SG expressed his wish earlier in the year to have a transitional government replace the current leadership. Before the SG leaves, he will make an announcement of the broad international support he has for his plan, and of the urgent need to set up a pretransition council to which authority can be transferred, now that Najibullah has made public his intention to resign. During the transition period there should be a general amnesty, an opening of major land routes, and provisions for the protection of personal property.

Benon believes that if Rabbani comes on board, the UN will be able to convene a conference before the end of April.

Platt says that the prime minister of Pakistan has several questions about the pretransition council, and about the transitional government. He wants to know who will be controlling what. Where will the real power be? [I consider these concerns to be diversionary. Clearly, Pakistan will benefit from anarchy once Najib leaves, so that its agents can seize power. Pakistan doesn't want an orderly transfer of power unless its clients can assume power.]

Benon agrees there are still questions to be resolved, such as who will control the army. Who is capable, and at the same time, inspires loyalty? Otherwise, there will be hordes of private militias. And the names on the list of Impartials must be capable people, not just names. That is why he is asking the different mujahidin groups to make nominations. They know who is capable, and their political support is indispensable. Benon warns: "Once this process breaks down, it will be a volcano. We will have to wait a long time for the dust to settle."

[Of all the comments I heard during and since my time in Afghanistan, these words were the most prophetic, the most vivid, and the most sincere. Benon knew very well whereof he spoke, and the fact that he had to witness the realization of his vision must have been a devastating personal experience.]

Our next stop is the European Community's (EC) mission. Benon is scheduled to brief them at 1300 hours.

He informs them of the U.S. government's intention to send ten thousand metric tons of wheat to Kabul. He adds that Iran has also promised to send food to Kabul. The price of food in Kabul, according to his sources, has gone down in the past few days.

Ever since the UN secretary-general's statement of 27 January, which outlined the UN's plans for a peaceful settlement to the conflict in Afghanistan, Benon has been trying to organize a Loya Jirga, he tells the EC. Najibullah's resignation was a step in this process. It advanced the process. The best option at this point is to constitute a Council of Impartials that will take full control and responsibility until a transition government can be arranged. The Loya Jirga will take place as soon as possible, within weeks. After that, a transitional government would last perhaps sixty days, long enough to be credible, but short enough to be transitional. Though it would be easiest to have the Loya Jirga inside Afghanistan, there are too many objections to that, and so the gathering will probably be held at a neutral location.

Benon then cites, as he did to Ambassador Platt, the elements that must be in place during the transition period: the opening of all major routes for transporting food and medicine, a general amnesty, guarantees for personal safety, and the protection of personal property. On the day of installation of the transitional government, there should be appropriate international recognition, to give it legitimacy. Pakistan and Iran have agreed to these proposals.

The secretary-general, Benon goes on, intends to inform the Security Council at once, so that these guarantees will have international support.

Najibullah has requested one thousand international peacekeeping troops to be stationed in Kabul, but Pakistan has reacted "violently" against that proposal. They feel there is no need for such a move.

[Pakistan, it is clear, wants forces sympathetic to Pakistan to capture Kabul and place in power a government it can control. International peacekeepers with their notorious predilection for impartiality would be an obstacle. Moreover, as a Muslim nation, Pakistan hates any hint of communism. Although communist parties are a legitimate element in Afghanistan's political landscape, and might reasonably be allowed to participate in any broad-based government of reconciliation, Pakistan will have none of it.

And since Pakistan's fierce anticommunist stance is supported by the United States, its wishes will be respected—no matter what the consequences. As Cordovez and Harrison say in their indispensable study, "for much of the war, American policy amounted to 'fighting to the last Afghan,' because the United States failed to couple its support for the mujahidin with support for the UN peace effort."[5]]

Benon says that although he does not think it possible to have one thousand UN peacekeepers inside Afghanistan, he does think it is necessary to have UN personnel at various points throughout the country in order to "observe" the transition. There are still elements supplying arms to military forces, in spite of an agreement to cease such supplies, he adds.

On the question of the size of the Council of Impartials, Benon says that he has never specified an exact number. "There should be between fifteen and twenty, so that some of them can be stationed outside Kabul."

Among the lists of proposed members for the Council that have been submitted, the Iranian list is more ethnically balanced, he continues. The Council must have wide representation if it is to have credibility. [In other words, I interpolate, the Council must include communists, pro-Iranian representatives, ethnic minorities, etc.]

A questioner asks if it is possible to hold any meetings inside Afghanistan while the armies, the various militias, are still armed. Benon replies that if the army is disarmed, there can be no law and order. They must agree on their responsibilities, but they cannot be disarmed.

[Benon notes that Rabbani is not yet "on board." He is still on the fence. "But my main concern is for Hekmatyar, who may feel he is losing and is threatened." [Gulbuddin Hekmatyar, a Pashtun and founder of the radical Hizbi-I-

Islami Party, has Pakistan's support, and hates the UN. He will not even talk to the UN, because he feels Benon is protecting Najibullah, and that the UN is willing to allow communist participation in a new Afghan government.]

Benon then expresses his hope that the EC will make a statement strongly endorsing his proposals, and make it clear there is no alternative at this point to the UN plan.

Asked about Najibullah, Benon says that Najib is willing to leave office. He wants only some assurance that the transfer of power will be orderly and not bloody.

———

9 April 1992

Benon has set up a meeting for me with the U.S. embassy in Islamabad. I am to speak with Janet Bogue, a political officer. Benon thinks it's a good idea for me to maintain contact with the U.S. embassy, especially since he is not always in Islamabad, and he wants the UN to keep the United States informed about what is going on in Kabul.

The United States is a major player in every conflict in the world, even when it is not a player, because the parties to a conflict want to know *why* the United States is not a player, and under what conditions it might become a player. In fact, parties to a conflict often include in their plans what actions it would take to keep the United States out, or to bring it in. From the standpoint of Washington, it is almost a lose-lose situation: if the United States remains on the sidelines, is it blamed for not using its considerable leverage to end a particular conflict. If it intervenes, it is accused of having hegemonistic ambitions.

While Benon speaks to the ambassador; I speak to the political officer. That is the protocol. I have no problem with that arrangement.

Janet Bogue is a pleasure to speak with. She is well informed, articulate, and professional, without being condescending as U.S. foreign service officers usually are, especially to members of the United Nations, and even more particularly to American members of the United Nations, whom they consider as creatures somewhere between beatniks and world socialists.

I ask her several questions. I ask how serious Platt was yesterday when he said the United States would do whatever it could to help the UN. Did she think it was right for the United States to place such confidence in the UN, or had that only been a polite thing to say? And why would the ambassador say he would do virtually anything to support the UN peace process when there was an ever-increasing likelihood that the process would collapse within a matter of days? I could not imagine the ambassador of France, or of the United Kingdom, saying: "Tell me what I can do to help." This must have been only a manner of speaking.

Bogue replies that the United States has no alternative at this point but to support the UN peace process. The United States is not prepared to take unilateral action. It does not want to become the world's policeman, and since the end of the Cold War, Afghanistan had been put on the back burner.

"But the United States sides with Pakistan," I offer. "Isn't that, in a manner of speaking, taking sides?"

"Pakistan is part of the UN peace process," she says, perfectly rehearsed.

"Does the U.S. have any policy goals in this area of the world?" I ask.

"The U.S. has three very definite concerns: stability for the entire region; cutting off the drug traffic; and helping to solve the refugee problem.

"And what if the UN peace plan collapses?" I ask.

"Our goals will remain the same. For now, since the only peace plan on the table is the UN plan, we support the UN plan. It is perfectly consistent with our goals."

———

Benon, as noted, has a different mandate than that of his predecessor, Diego Cordovez. Cordovez, who negotiated the accords that oversaw the withdrawal of Soviet troops from Afghanistan, was allowed only to speak with governments. The UN is an intergovernmental organization, and its member states, until recently, have always considered it proper to conduct negotiations only among recognized governments. That practice is codified in Article II, paragraph 7 of the UN Charter, which states: "Nothing contained in the present Charter shall authorize the United Nations to intervene in matters which are essentially within the domestic jurisdiction of any state."

But that respect for sovereignty first began to crack under the injustices of apartheid. The international community did not feel it could stand idly by in the face of such genocidal policies. The Security Council felt it had to join the struggle against apartheid, if not with troops, then at least with economic sanctions, and with moral and political support for the foes of apartheid. To do that, it decided that apartheid was a threat to international security, in that its practices destabilized an entire region. Once the Cold War ended, the Security Council was able, with much less diffidence, to extend its intervention to domestic disputes. It no longer had to rationalize that a civil war threatened an entire region. Such arguments were self-evident, given the fact that money, commerce, information, and even military advisors cross borders every day in virtually every part of the world. The question of military interven-

tion thus became a political one, rather than a philosophi-
cal one: Did the Council have the will [i.e., the votes]? And
would member states supply the troops?

Following the collapse of the Soviet Union [and its new
reluctance to use its veto power in the Security Council],
the UN was able to intervene in civil strife in Somalia,
Angola, Afghanistan, and Yugoslavia. In the case of Afghanistan, however, Russia still disapproved of the Security
Council's involvement in domestic matters, since it didn't
want to set a precedent for what might one day lead to
Security Council intervention in civil strife in Russia's
southern, Muslim provinces. Thus, it refused to agree to a
Security Council mandate to intervene in Afghanistan.
Instead, it agreed to allow the UN secretary-general to use
his "good offices" to try to bring peace to the region. Even
then, however, the Russians and others insisted on desig-
nating the secretary-general's mission in Afghanistan as
one of an international, rather than domestic, character.
Thus, the mission I joined was designated The Office of the
Secretary-General in Afghanistan and Pakistan (OSGAP).
And of course the Russians had a point. Much of the war in
Afghanistan was being directed from across the border in
Pakistan. Weapons, soldiers, and supplies were moving
across the border from Pakistan into Afghanistan at the
same time that tens of thousands of hapless refugees were
moving in the opposite direction.

In fact, the collapse of the Soviet Union and the realign-
ment of forces within the UN Security Council created an
unprecedented opportunity for the UN secretary-general to
take new initiatives. NATO had yet to define its new identity in the wake of its obsolescence as a defensive alliance,
and the former communist countries suddenly had no uni-
fying principle. Correspondingly, there was an organiza-
tional power vacuum of sorts at the UN. Although the

Security Council was expected to act with near unanimity once the Cold War ended, the scope of its competence was still to be tested. Into the breach leapt the secretary-general. More than ever before, the secretary-general emerged as a desirable complement to the mandates of the Security Council and the ambitions of regional organizations such as NATO.[6]

Benon's mission in Afghanistan was a case in point. As the secretary-general's personal representative in Afghanistan, he was able to take creative initiatives on short notice, without having to seek the Security Council's approval each time. His efforts under those conditions were monumental. Of course, Benon never avoided or eschewed contact with the major powers. He was not an independent contractor on a secret mission. But by acting in the context of the secretary-general's good offices, he was spared the slow and agonizing formality of having to await a Security Council resolution at each bend in the road. In the end, Benon's task was hopeless and thankless, but it was much less costly or politically contentious than Security Council intervention would have been.

After lunch, I meet with Huntley Anderson, Benon's chief political adviser. Anderson is a lawyer with a Jamaican passport, though he has not lived in Jamaica for almost three decades. He has been in the UN for a good while. He is bright and eccentric, but not on good terms with Benon. He is supposed to brief me.

There are always personality clashes in politics, as in business, and my own attitude in such cases is to try to concentrate on ideological differences. Because Benon is head of mission, most of the office sides with him in his dispute with Anderson. In fact, most of the office shuns

Anderson. Meanwhile, Anderson constantly writes memos to Benon, advising him on possible courses of action. Anderson thinks he is a genius, and the more Benon ignores him, the more convinced Anderson is that his own ideas are brilliant.

But there is an added dimension to their dispute. For the past several months, Anderson has been sending to Gianni Picco at UN headquarters in New York copies of the memos he writes to Benon, a tactic that inevitably undermines cohesion and morale in the mission. Picco is the point man in New York for Afghanistan, and Benon is the only one in the mission who is supposed to communicate directly with him or the secretary-general. That is the protocol. Meanwhile, although Picco is a long-time colleague of Benon's, the two have become rivals in recent months. Picco was tied very closely to former secretary-general Pérez de Cuéllar, while Benon is the personal representative of the new SG, Boutros-Ghali. Benon's star is rising, while Picco's is in decline. Anderson, more out of frustration and personal ambition than out of disloyalty, tries to exploit this rivalry. He complains constantly that Benon will not listen to his advice.

Meanwhile, Benon's response to Anderson's mischief has been to freeze him out of the picture even more. He doesn't show him copies of cables that he sends to New York, he avoids inviting him to meetings, and doesn't discuss strategy with him. Since Benon doesn't trust Anderson, he doesn't keep him informed of various activities.

As to their ideological differences, Anderson tells me during his briefing that he believes Benon is trying to keep Najib in power, not so much for political reasons, but because Benon feels an obligation to protect him, having convinced him to resign. Yet Najibullah is playing Benon for a fool, Anderson believes. Najib should have been out of

Kabul long ago. He will hang on to power as long as he can. Benon's commitment to Najib has rendered the UN ineffective, Anderson tells me. [Colleagues tell me that Anderson also carries this message to the various embassies in Islamabad. He tells them that Benon is pro-Najibullah, and that this allegiance has diminished the UN's leverage. But ironically, in the world of political labels, Anderson is not considered either disruptive or idiosyncratic; he is considered pro-Pakistani.]

Anderson tells me that the way to replace Najib with an interim authority is to appeal to the front-line states, mainly Pakistan. The various groups inside Afghanistan are too disorganized; they will never agree on anything. Pakistan, Iran, Turkey, and others are the ones who can provide a stable transition.

What I consider the most important point in Anderson's briefing is his analysis of how Benon and the UN are perceived: as being pro-Najibullah. If that is true, and it may be, then it is a liability. At the same time, that view is a misperception, no doubt fueled by the domestic agendas of various players. There is no doubt that Benon—and UN officials in New York all the way up to the secretary-general—feel a political obligation to make good on their promise to bring an impartial transitional authority to replace Najib. That was the understanding when Najib resigned, and the UN worked very hard to convince him to resign. Yet, it is also true that the mujahidin now fighting the Afghan government do not want a transitional authority that would retain any hint of power for Najib or his followers. They consider Najib a pawn of the Soviet Union.

Najib, on the other hand, is not at this point concerned with retaining power. He knows he cannot. What he fears is that Afghanistan will be taken over by fundamentalists and/or by its traditional enemy, Pakistan. For what it is

worth, Najib's communist government was secular, nationalistic, and dominated by Pashtun. He does not want to see a
new authority that will surrender Afghan independence,
become a religious state, or discriminate against the Pashtun.

As for Benon, he feels obligated to implement UN policy. I sincerely believe he does not take sides. Anyhow, he
couldn't if he wanted to, because there are too many sides.
Afghanistan is a polygon of perverse political intrigue, not
a simple dichotomy. At the same time, I can understand
how much any UN official might want to see Afghanistan
remain independent, and not be under any other nation's
thumb. In that sense, many of us in the mission are Afghan
nationalists.

[Though it may seem naïve, mystical, even presumptu-
ous, to think of oneself as a nationalist in a country torn by
civil strife, especially after having arrived for the first time
only a few weeks before, that was how I felt. And the dis-
tinctness of that feeling was a tribute to the depth, warmth,
and strength of the Afghans I had met. An Afghan who
places his hand over his heart as a way of greeting you, in
fact touches the heart of the person he meets. It is hard to
find a country with a more majestic landscape, and with
people who are tougher, more sentimental, more generous,
and have been more brutalized. In my very limited experience I have seldom met anyone who has visited Afghanistan who disliked the country or the people. Quite to the
contrary, virtually everyone I know who has been to Afghanistan liked it and wanted to return.

As for Benon's relationship with Najib, it is a complex
one. Najib likes Benon, because he sees the UN as Afghanistan's last hope against subjugation by fundamentalist
forces led by Pakistan. He also likes Benon personally.
Benon, on the other hand, has been so instrumental in
implementing the UN's policy of having Najib resign that

he feels responsible for Najib's safety. This responsibility, as I have said before, is not a moral responsibility; it is a political responsibility.]

I thank Anderson for his briefing. Though I am not sympathetic to his political views, I take him seriously. He is bright and energetic.

———

Benon himself is an unusual personality. Above all, he has presence. If the UN's venture into Afghanistan in the early 1990s were ever to be made into a film, which one hopes will never happen, Benon would have to play himself. No one else could make him credible. He is a heavy, broad-shouldered, extroverted Armenian from Cyprus, who speaks Turkish, along with fractured English, French, and a few other languages, a true international creation, a rambling polyglot who chain smokes, bullies, and charms his way into the heart of almost anyone who has the patience to endure him. Like a true Mediterranean, he speaks with his hands, his eyes, and his body movements. His manner is always unconventional, whether he is among diplomats, junior staff, or top UN officials. He is simultaneously loud, insulting, obscene, funny, sentimental, generous, shrewd, and practical. He can reduce the most difficult political problem to a simple obscenity, and usually he is right in his analysis. "What are the different factions fighting for in Afghanistan?" someone once asked him. "Dope," he replied. "What exactly does the opposition want from Najib?" a newcomer on the scene once asked him. "His balls," Benon replied.

He is also a man of his word. In Afghanistan, Benon has credibility with all sides. Which is to say that all sides trust/mistrust him equally. They trust him because he is direct and speaks in images they can apprehend, in basic metaphors that transcend interpretation. And they mistrust him because they are all paranoid, and they mistrust everybody.

He has boundless energy. I have seen Benon work twenty-hour days on almost no sleep. Generally, he works seven days a week, and expects the same from his staff. He moves among Kabul, Peshawar, Islamabad, and Teheran with dogged intensity, on a kind of nicotine high, but never out of control. Those close to him voice fear for his health, but Benon seems immune to illness. He is a motor in the body of a man.

At the same time, Benon is aware that he is a major international figure in an accelerating tragedy that threatens very soon to play itself out in a paroxysm of anarchy, chaos, and bloody revenge. One recalls Yeats: "The best lack all conviction, while the worst / Are full of passionate intensity." The worst are all around Kabul, poised to strike. The worst are also in power in Kabul, waiting to be struck.

The few weeks before I arrived, as well as the days since I arrived, have been, understandably, a time of great tension for Benon. He knows very well that the time bomb is ticking. He is not one to deceive himself. And he is agitated, impatient. At times he seems like a cornered animal, a wounded bear; at other times like an angry champion about to lose his title belt. The trappings of his dubious influence are slipping away, and he knows it. The more appeals made to him by a dying Afghan government, the more powerless to act and the more marginal he becomes. And the more appeals he makes to the various mujahidin factions, the more antagonistic to them he seems. Under such conditions, what one comes to admire in his efforts is that he continues the fight, even though he suspects he cannot win. Because what is at stake here is not merely honor. It is not a matter of how one plays the game, no matter who wins. Such attitudes belong on a college campus. No, here and now in Afghanistan, winning is the only thing that matters, because winning means being able to avert human slaughter. What drives Benon, what drives most of us here, is the greatest high of all, one I have already mentioned—the remote chance of being able to save lives. There are truly not many situations in life when one can actually feel he has the opportunity to save human lives—not simply one life, as in the case of a physician, but hundreds, perhaps thousands, of lives. Benon knows he has that chance now. Perhaps that is the ultimate vanity, to think one can act to save thousands of lives, using little more than the force of his personality. But if that attitude be vanity, then it is a far more humane strain than the more common one of self-aggrandizement.

12 April 1992

Military briefing at OSGAP headquarters in Kabul. We are eight people. Five military officers, headed by Colonel Patrick Nowlan of Ireland, OSGAP's chief military advisor, and three civilians, including myself. Colonel Nowlan informs us that rumors of a political settlement have brought prices down drastically. The exchange rate for the U.S. dollar has been cut in half, from 1,800 Afghans to the dollar to 900 Afghans to the dollar. There is news that food has arrived in the capital.

Because of fighting around the city, electrical power supplies are uncertain. There was no heat last night in many homes. We ourselves are urged to use electric heaters. Lights blink on and off, radios go on and off. We cannot be sure of power supplies.

At night, packs of dogs are reported roaming the streets.

There are legendary tales about the dogs of Kabul. There have been times when they virtually overran the city, and all but ruled the streets. At such times, so the stories go, government officials put out poisoned meat to attract and kill them. That is how officials thin the ranks of stray dogs. And with men going off to war, and families leaving the country as refugees, dogs are sometimes abandoned. They are, after all, another mouth to feed.

The dogs on the streets now, however, are not "attack" dogs, Colonel Nowlan says. But since rabies exists in Kabul, he cautions us to drive at night, not to walk.

Imagine that. In New York we are told not to wander in the parks at night because of perverts, criminals, junkies. In Kabul, during wartime, it is the dogs to fear. The dogs of war, one might say.

---

13 April 1992

Benon has a meeting at 10 a.m. with the National Salvation Society, a high-level group of Afghan intellectuals. Avni Botsali and I accompany him. [Avni is a Turkish diplomat seconded to the UN for this mission. He serves, more or less, as Benon's deputy. He speaks Dari—Afghan Persian—one of the two official languages of Afghanistan.] The Society makes suggestions for transferring power once Najib resigns. They suggest that the Council of Impartials should meet with the current administration in the office of the President, in the presence of the UN. The army and current government institutions should declare their allegiance to the Council. One of the vice-presidents in the current government can become a member of the Council.

In accordance with the Afghan Constitution, the speakers say, Najib could declare his inability to perform his duties, and power would be transferred to the first deputy vice-president, who would become a member of the Council. The vice-president would act as a link between the current government and the Council. The Council could then suspend the Constitution, suspend the parliament, declare a state of emergency, and elect a head of the Council. Legislative power would pass to the Council under the provisions of a state of emergency. Next, the cabinet would resign, but members would be asked by the Council to continue, with the exception of controversial figures, who would be replaced. The armed forces would remain in place. The Supreme Court would resign, and then be appointed *ad interim*. In this way, the Council would have both legislative and executive powers.

We take note of the proposal. In calmer times, such a proposal might be possible to enact. The speakers are making concrete suggestions for an orderly, constitutional transfer of power. But, as the saying goes, they seem to be rearranging deck chairs while the *Titanic* is sinking. No one has any idea how the fall of Kabul will play out, how orderly or disorderly it will be, what will or will not be possible. The anxiety level is high. Those with a tradition of poisoning stray dogs are certainly capable of murdering political undesirables.

Next, we have a conversation with Ali Akbar Popal, a Pashtun nationalist. We visit him at his home. The UN stays in touch with as many sources as possible. It is the only way to get a broad sense of what is happening, or what might happen. Popal is a respected Kabul intellectual, a middle-aged man. He offers us tea. He is always hospitable and respectful. Whether or not he feels personally threatened is hard to tell. How much he is identified with

Najibullah is also hard to tell. But a power vacuum has a way of sucking everyone into the vortex of anarchy.

Popal is composed, but anxious. He does not want to see Kabul destroyed. He does not want to see the Pashtun lose their dominance. He does not want Afghanistan to be under Pakistan's thumb. These are his broad concerns. But today he expresses what he says are three specific worries of the people here in Kabul. First, personal security. They fear looting, rape, a complete loss of law and order. [Police, the guardians of law and order, have been among the most ruthless of Najib's allies. Will the people turn on them? Will the police flee? And if they flee, who will protect the citizens and their property?]

Popal's second item is amnesty. Will a general amnesty cover all, including criminals? Will convicted felons be let out of jail?

Third, what about the economy? If the Council of Impartials is to last only forty-five days, as he has heard, until an interim government can be appointed, what happens to the economy? Who pays the civil servants? The Afghan people don't want to wait another forty-five days for action. Or for their salaries. They want to know from the first day that something is being done about the economy. Civil servants haven't been paid for months. People have no money to buy bread.

[Popal is a bright man. His questions are practical. But I have to wonder if he actually believes that the UN can do anything about the impending doom that hangs over Kabul. He knows, he must know, that hope at this point is thinner than a Pentium chip, and stores much less practical information. At times like this, however, the UN becomes more a secular god, an *ad hoc* savior, than a reality to those desperate souls who have no alternative. We are, I keep telling myself, only a handful of unarmed people in a fractured country of thousands of heavily armed and vengeful warriors. How can we possibly stop anything? But I cannot say that to Popal.]

On the issue of security, Benon says he will bring it up again, as he has in the past, to the mujahidin groups in Peshawar that are deciding on the Council of Impartials. On the point of amnesty, that is for the new authorities to decide, but every society makes a distinction between common felons and political criminals. The third point, managing the economy, is under discussion at the international level among aid agencies, and will be an urgent concern of the new Council, he is sure.

Late this afternoon Benon leaves for Peshawar.

14 April 1992

1100 hours. Avni Botsali and I meet with Abdul Wakil, the foreign minister, and Dauoud Kawyan, deputy foreign minister. Wakil confirms that Massoud's forces have taken Charikar and Jabalussaraj, in Parwan Province to the north of Kabul, from government forces. Wakil has been in contact with them, trying to make a deal concerning the future of Kabul. He is urging restraint. All of the government's armed forces have also been urged to restrain themselves. Massoud is putting pressure on Bagram Air Base, a military facility twenty to twenty-five miles north of Kabul. Massoud is confident he can take Bagram before Hekmatyar can. That would put Massoud in a good position to enter Kabul. [But Massoud, a Tajik, has said he does not want to take Kabul, which has a majority Pashtun population. Hekmatyar is Pashtun. The people of Kabul, however, are ambiguous in their attitude toward Hekmatyar. Though Hekmatyar is Pashtun, he is supported by Pakistan, whom the Afghan people hate.]

Wakil says he had offered weeks ago to go to speak to Massoud in order to make a deal. But Najibullah had refused to let him go. Wakil said that Massoud is a hero of Afghanistan because he stood up the Soviets when few others did. He deserved respect. [Recently, Najibullah had sent Kamaluddin Izhaqzzi, president of the National Mediation Commission, to speak to Massoud, but the meeting did not produce any results. Perhaps Najibullah would not let Wakil go because he feared Wakil would defect. Wakil is a Tajik like Massoud. He is also a second cousin to Babrak Karmal, whom Najib deposed.]

Wakil says Massoud will continue his offensive so long as Najib remains in Kabul. If Wakil were allowed to see Massoud, he would tell him that he should support the UN plan to transfer power to a Council of Impartials as the only hope of avoiding anarchy in Kabul. Massoud has always said he would not enter Kabul, that he does not want bloodshed, and that he will keep pressure against Kabul only so long as Najibullah remains there. Everyone has good relations with Massoud, Wakil says. In Parwan province, everything is calm; shops are open, roads are open. Two towns in the north recently fell to Massoud without any bloodshed. They made deals.

Massoud has twenty thousand troops around Kabul, Wakil says. Massoud is concerned about a message he received from Peshawar saying that Hekmatyar had infiltrated Kabul with some Khalqs. [The Khalqs are Pashtun nationalists loyal to Karmal. They have a reputation for being brutal. They have never forgiven Najib for deposing Karmal. Karmal, a communist like Najib, still has many followers in Afghan political circles. Massoud, meanwhile, is anticommunist.] Wakil stresses that Benon should come to Kabul *today*! Perhaps his presence might prevent bloodshed. [Benon is in Peshawar, trying to negotiate the formation of the Council of Impartials.]

————

1400 hours. Avni and I meet with First Deputy Defense Minister and Commander of the Kabul Garrison, General Mohammed Nabil Azimi. Azimi is a broadshouldered, heavyset man, over six feet tall, with thick black hair and a rectangular face. He is a Tajik. He confirms that the Second Division (government forces) have joined [i.e., defected to] Massoud, and that Massoud is now in control of Jabalussarraj and Charikar to the north. In Bagram, the situation is stable. There have been one or two offensives against Bagram Air Base, but they have been repulsed.

Azimi says he has moved government reserve troops around the defense perimeter of Kabul. He has sent reinforcements to Bagram Air Base. He is in communication with the former government forces that went over to Massoud when he took Charikar. They were satisfied with their situation, and preferred to be there rather than in Kabul. Azimi said he had no intention of starting operations against areas that had gone over to the mujahidin. He preferred to remain in contact with them and to convince them to support the UN peace plan. [First of all, Azimi doubted he could win back areas that had already fallen to the mujahidin. Second, he did not want to disperse his troops any more widely than he had to. He wanted them to remain in Kabul. Third, he was afraid that his troops might defect if they left the capital. Fourth, he hoped to leave himself the option of going over to the other side in case Kabul should be overrun. Losers, even potential losers, always support the UN. Winners ignore it until after their victory, and then seek its endorsement to legitimize their victory.]

During Massoud's takeover of Charikar, Azimi informs us, there was almost no fighting. Government forces only fired one Scud rocket. There was no direct combat.

When Benon returns to Kabul, Azimi tells us, he would like to talk to him in private. He has his own idea of how he believes the peace process should proceed. First, resignation of the president. Second, establishment of a military council to control the armed forces. Third, transfer of political power to the Council of Impartials, and departure of the president. All government ministers should also leave, along with the president. Once the Council of Impartials was established, the army would follow the instructions of the Council.

1430 hours. Avni and I meet with General Baha, military and civilian governor of Kabul.

General Baha observes that there is now a coalition in Charikar and Jabalussaraj, under Massoud, similar to the one in Mazar-i-Sharif in the north, under General Abdul Rashid Dostom. [Charikar is not that far from Kabul, about seventy-five kilometers due north. Mazar-i-Sharif is much farther from Kabul, several hundred kilometers north northwest, and backed up to the border with Uzbekistan. Dostom is Uzbek, and though he is respected as a warrior, he does not have Massoud's inspirational following, or Massoud's outstanding political sense. At the same time, the Uzbeks are reputed to be the fiercest of all Afghan fighters; some call them the Prussians of Asia].

Though Hekmatyar and Massoud are both threatening Bagram Air Base, Baha continues, he does not anticipate a military offensive against Kabul. As a Tajik, Massoud might be able to form coalitions outside Kabul, but inside Kabul he would face resistance from the Pashtun. Massoud knows that. He does not want to enter Kabul; he simply wants to prevent it from falling to Hekmatyar. [I have now heard this opinion so many times, that Massoud would not enter Kabul because it is a Pashtun city, that I begin to disbelieve it. It has become a mantra. Perhaps Massoud *would* enter Kabul.]

Baha asks us if Sevan has announced the fifteen members of the Council of Impartials. When we say he has not, Baha expresses his disappointment. [Actually, each announcement of a military development, such as the fall of Charikar and Jabalussaraj, or the pressure on Bagram Air Base, is a disincentive for the formation of a civilian leadership. As in every war, it is usually the military leaders who call the shots, since progress on the battlefield provides leverage for political leaders. And since the battlefield situation is still fluid, none of the political leaders wants to commit himself to compromises that may be reversed in a day or two by developments in the field—which is why, ideally, there should be a cease-fire *before* political negotiations begin. But such luxuries are not possible here and now in Afghanistan. Instead, as odds rise that Kabul may come under siege, all the various players are dodging, squirming, running for position, and for their lives. It is a game of musical chairs, except that the chairs are hot seats.]

Baha believes that the statement by Najibullah on 18 March that he intended to resign weakened the state. It is imperative to know where and when the transfer of power will take place. With so many forces massed around Kabul, he questions whether fifteen people can have very much power, or keep law and order.

He fears that Massoud's coalition is trying to impose a solution on Kabul. He also fears that groups led by Hekmatyar, massed south and east of Kabul are planning to attack Jalalabad and Gardez and then enter Kabul. Everyone knows that Hekmatyar rejects the UN plan.

Baha believes that Hekmatyar may attempt to attack Kabul as soon as tomorrow, perhaps from Logar. But he predicts that Hekmatyar will fail because Kabul's defenses, still under government control, have been adequately reinforced. [I seriously doubted this last remark. Kabul had no defenses. It had little more than defections and prayers.]

He believes that the UN, which took such a strong position against Iraq during the Gulf War, should make a strong declaration to all belligerents in Afghanistan to respect the peace process, because if the UN plan failed, armed groups would attack the cities and there would be anarchy and slaughter. The UN should also tell belligerents to abandon all ideas of partition. The UN should make clear that it intended to protect the territorial integrity of Afghanistan.

He tells us that he proposed at a meeting of the Central Committee that all members of the Committee should retain their positions until the end of the emergency. After that, they can remain in their houses until a new authority takes charge. If all those who were controversial were to flee, there might be panic. When it was time for them to leave, they could leave discretely.

[General Baha was clearly nervous and felt threatened. He was tied to Najibullah, whose hours, whose minutes, were numbered. But Baha's logic was illogical, his reason was unreasonable, and his analogies were incongruous. He was a man whose life was in serious danger, and he was appealing to the UN to save him, to exert powers the UN never had or would have, not even under peaceful circumstances. To suggest that the UN, with only a handful of unarmed military observers on the ground could "take charge" at this point was preposterous, as was his wish that an orderly transition of power might obtain. The analogy to the Gulf War was frivolous. In Iraq, the multinational force—which had the Security Council's endorsement, but was *not* a UN force—had numbered 500,000 well-armed individuals. It was able to "take charge." Moreover, it had taken six months to assemble.

At the same time, Baha's pride would not allow him to appeal directly to the UN to save his life. He would not ask for asylum. That would be dishonorable. And he could not go over to the other side. He had too many skeletons in his closet. As for his appeal that the UN should insist on the territorial integrity of Afghanistan, *that* had merit, but was largely academic at this point. The various military factions had already carved up Afghanistan. They were not asking for partition or annexation to a neighboring country, because they already had effective autonomy in their regions. And the Coalition of the North—Massoud, Dostom, et al.—was mainly to oppose Hekmatyar, perhaps eventually to take over all of Afghanistan intact; it was certainly not intent on dividing Afghanistan in half. The battle at this point was for Kabul. In fact, Baha was more concerned about the threat from outside Afghanistan than from inside. He resented the interference of Pakistan and Iran. He feared that the three million Afghan refugees in Pakistan and/or the two million more in Iran might be shaped into an invasion force that would deliver Afghanistan into the arms of one of its neighbors. He feared that possibility more than he feared the Coalition of the North.]

[And of course he was right. What came to be known as the Taliban a few years later was just the type of force Baha and other Afghan patriots had feared. The Taliban were, in fact, Afghans; but they were under the thumb of Pakistan, and were reinforced on the ground by thousands of Pakistani, Arab and other mercenaries.]

—————

15 April 1992

0730 hours. Avni informs us at this morning's briefing that Bagram Air Base fell last night, almost without a fight, to Massoud.

According to Colonel Nowlan, the defenses of Kabul are a joke. Moreover, since Bagram is a military air base, the mujahidin now have an air capability for the first time.

Avni tells us that Najib called this morning at 12:30 a.m. (half an hour after midnight), asking for an immediate convening of the Council of Impartials. He also wants Benon to pick him up at once in the UN plane, and fly him safely out of the country.

Though Kabul is virtually defenseless, life in the streets is calm. Colonel Nowlan cautions against alarmist rhetoric. He says we must know accurately and rationally what the situation is like in Kabul. He decries recent reports in the international press about hysteria in Kabul. [I recall a few days ago that a British reporter told me that he gets a bonus any time his story is the lead story on the hourly newscast. I marvel again at the incentives for hysteria and disinformation in the fourth estate.]

Benon is supposed to arrive this afternoon in Kabul, from Islamabad.

—————

The activity around me seems almost surreal. All this talk of disaster, of a capital about to fall, of air bases being captured, of perimeter defenses that don't exist, of soldiers changing allegiances, of wild dogs patrolling the streets at night. Yet the small world I move in from day to day seems quite safe. It is run by internationals and supported by local Afghans, a kind of settler colonialism in the cause of peace. And what stimulates the adrenaline here and now are hope and determination—positive forces; not anxiety, dread, danger.

In fact, I really don't feel threatened. Inconvenienced, yes, because my freedom of movement is restricted, and my living conditions are often less than elegant. But I don't feel threatened, physically afraid. I wonder how I seem to the Afghans I deal with every day: the generals, the servants, the interpreters. Privileged, no doubt. A source of hope, perhaps. A foreigner, for sure. Can they feel my positive energy?

———

We listen to the BBC constantly. Their world news roundup reflects the priorities of the international community, and by extension, those of the UN.

First item: The United States and the United Kingdom are demanding that two men from Libya, accused of blowing up a passenger jet flying over Lockerbie, Scotland, should be sent to the United States or the United Kingdom for trial. If not, the UN Security Council is prepared to adopt sanctions against Libya. [On December 21, 1988, 270 people were killed when Pan Am 103 was blown from the sky.]

Second item: More fighting in Bosnia and Herzegovina. The United States is threatening the Serbs. [Oil is apparently thicker than blood. Bosnian Muslims are supported by Saudi Arabia, the world's largest oil producer. By supporting the Bosnian Muslims, the United States can show it is not anti-Muslim, and it can maintain good relations with Saudi Arabia. At the same time, NATO can push its borders eastward by bringing Bosnia under its mailed wing.]

Third item: Iraq. Iraq has fallen from grace since its invasion of Kuwait. Though NATO once supported Iraq in its dirty, drawn-out war against Iran, Iraq is now officially a bad guy in the cowboy world of American foreign policy. The United States is warning Iraq not to starve the Kurds in its northern region, and to halt its blockade of food supplies to that area. Iraq must also continue to dismantle its facilities for making weapons of mass destruction and allow international inspection to verify the results. Or else.

Beyond these three items, I speculate, there is major concern in the U.S. and in Europe about the mounting problems of the Commonwealth of Independent States (CIS): Russia, the Ukraine, and Belarus. President Yeltsin's proposed economic reforms are being rebuffed by hardliners in his parliament, who say he is going too fast. His cabinet has resigned. If Yeltsin is prevented from instituting economic reforms, then the international loans promised him by the world banking system, amounting to $24 billion at this point, will be jeopardized.

Russia is a major concern for the U.S. at all times, because it is a nuclear power. South America, because of its proximity to the United States, is also a major concern. If its economies collapse, the U.S. will be flooded with more immigrants, and United States banks will lose billions of dollars in loans. The Middle East is always a concern for the United States because of oil, and because of strategic considerations; even if the oil fields in Arabia ran dry, the area would be important geopolitically. China is important. Japan is important. In fact, now that Russian troops are out of Afghanistan, Afghanistan's problems are quite low on the priority lists of the United States, NATO, and by extension, the UN. Those are the realities.

Then there is still debate about whether the UN has the right under the Charter to intervene *within* a country to protect threatened minorities. Military intervention needs some legal cover in order not to look like brazen imperialism. Can the international community use military force to protect the Kurds in Iraq, but not in Turkey? The Muslims in Bosnia, but not in China? Would it respond if the Uzbeks claimed they were a persecuted minority in Afghanistan? But these questions are academic now. Even if the UN Security Council did want to intervene militarily in Afghanistan, it would take the Council days to arrive at a decision, and months, under enormous risk, to bring in the necessary force, whereas Kabul is destined to fall within days. Afghanistan has effectively been abandoned by the international community, a case of political triage. It is doomed.

At this point, Massoud seems unstoppable. The question is, will Hekmatyar accept Massoud's dominance, or will he choose to battle Massoud, either by taking Kabul or by circumventing the city and assaulting Massoud's positions to the north? And will Massoud enter Kabul, even though he has said he would not?

There is also the threat of ethnic and factional warfare within Kabul. Will the Khalqi, who support Babrak Karmal, move against Najib's people? The Khalqi are in Kabul. Some have never left, some have infiltrated among the refugees seeking asylum. Or, will the Pashtun in Kabul move against the non-Pashtun, whose refugees continue to swell Kabul, and who are virtually in control of certain neighborhoods?

Meanwhile, civil services have all but broken down. A few buses are running, but other services are spotty. Civil servants are not being paid. Like others, they are considering whether to defect, and if so, where to go, whom to join.

This is what anarchy is all about—to feel a victim in your own home, in your own city, to have nobody to whom you can appeal, to feel you are a twenty-four-hour target for reasons that may exist only in the mind of an anonymous attacker, a neighbor, a former friend. *Things fall apart, the center cannot hold* (Yeats).

———

1030 hours. Briefing by Colonel Nowlan. Be sure that all vehicles are fueled, in good working order, and are flying a UN flag. When using radios, use only call signs and house numbers. No names. Be sure to know alternate routes to the airport in case we must evacuate. Bring a backpack to work, with enough to sustain you for a few days: socks, underwear, toiletries, clothes, raincoat, etc. Check BBC news every morning at 0500 and 0530. Everyone should have, or have access to, a shortwave radio.

We discuss where we will assemble for evacuation. There are several collection points. Each person is responsible for knowing his collection point.

———

1130 hours. Avni and I go to visit General Yar Mohammed. I have no idea what the general's responsibilities are, but at this point it doesn't matter. No one can exercise his responsibilities now. We simply stay in touch to see what information the general has.

He tells us that eleven of the fifteen members for the proposed Council of Impartials were approved this morning in Peshawar. And there is a coalition government in Bagram, which fell yesterday to Massoud. No reports of violence there. No reports of arrests. A deal was struck.

Hekmatyar's forces are on the move to the south of Kabul. They may be assembling for an offensive on Kabul.

The general wants to do anything possible to prevent violence in Kabul. Massoud's forces, which took Charikar and Bagram, have said they had no intention of entering Kabul. He believes them. The problem is Hekmatyar. We have heard this refrain before, but each time we hear it again the speaker seems more desperate.

Yesterday, the Afghan government decided to establish contact with forces to the north, loosely known as the Coalition of the North, or the Northern Alliance, an alliance between Massoud and Dostom. Today official directives will be released saying that government forces should join the predominantly mujahidin forces to the north, in order to prevent bloodshed, and to promote the UN peace plan.

[The real alliance, I think, has been between desperation and absurdity. Imagine: a government directive ordering its troops to desert and join the enemy, in order to promote a peace plan that the enemy has already rejected. And who will enforce the UN peace plan? A handful of unarmed UN military observers?]

Last night, General Yar Mohammed continues, the executive committee of the Watan (Homeland) Party decided that government forces should not take military action without direct orders from the president [who has already announced his intention to resign, who has very little power outside of Kabul, and virtually no power within Kabul]. A group was sent to contact General Massoud to tell him that plans for air strikes against the Northern Alliance have been canceled. [Now that Bagram Air Base has been captured by Massoud, how could government planes carry out an air strike anyhow? Where would they fly from? And who would fly the planes? The pilots have deserted.]

The general says that once agreement on a number of issues has been reached with the Northern Alliance, the government will attempt to make agreement with forces to the east and south of the capital. These forces are largely responsible to Hekmatyar. Meanwhile, General Azimi is in charge of the defense of Kabul.

Last night half a dozen rockets were launched toward Kabul by Hekmatyar's forces. General Yar Mohammed says he hopes this will not be the beginning of a siege of Kabul. He sincerely hopes that Mr. Sevan will be able to bring about a peaceful settlement to this conflict. The general would be quite happy if the same arrangement could be made for Kabul that was made for the northern cities. There should be a coalition between government forces and forces of the Northern Alliance. No bloodshed, no revenge.

[Of course we do not know that there has been no bloodshed in the northern cities, but I suspect it is true. Massoud is a very good politician and has numerous reasons for not punishing government troops. First of all, government forces are mostly "grunts," or conscripts, with no particular obligation to Najibullah. Massoud would rather have them as allies than as corpses. As for the officer corps, they know very well how the war is going, and they are quite willing to surrender. Besides, most of the government forces are Pashtun, and if Massoud starts to execute Pashtun soldiers, then he invites retaliation against own ethnic Tajiks, many of whom are seeking refuge within Kabul. But Massoud is as clever as he is charismatic. He wants allegiance more than revenge. He knows there are times when trust and respect can be more a source of power than weapons.]

General Yar Mohammed thinks a coalition between government forces and the Northern Alliance is already possible within certain districts in Kabul. In fact, negotiations are ongoing at this moment with that goal in mind.

However, he fears a rivalry between Hekmatyar and Massoud. He heard that Hekmatyar had received orders last night from his political leaders in Peshawar to attack Massoud, but that his soldiers refused to obey the order. They didn't want more bloodshed. The international community must prevent military rivalries inside Kabul. Hekmatyar is dangerous.

Finally, General Yar Mohammed tells us that the government's minister of interior affairs has reached an agreement with leaders of the Khalqi, Karmal's followers, that they would participate in a coalition along with the Watan Party (Najib's party) and others. [I doubt if they reached agreement, or if they did, whether the agreement would be honored by either side.]

1500 hours. Meeting with the National Salvation Society. The general who greets us tells us of his concerns. [I could never have imagined so many generals in such a small country. Their names bob in a sea of confusion in my irreverent mind. I do not even know the name of the speaker.] Developments have occurred, he says, that he had expected would happen only *after* the peace process had begun. For example, government forces north of the capital have defected to Massoud. That alliance should have taken place only after the peace process had begun. Then that development would have been acceptable. Now it was merely a defection, a sign of disarray.

The government's army is completely demoralized. Conditions are very bad. Kabul authorities are not strong enough to control the situation. If the Council of Impartials arrives in Kabul, perhaps they can control the situation. Otherwise, anarchy. He fears that there are too many ethnic and political groups within Kabul to permit a deal to be struck as it was in the northern cities and in Bagram. At this point Hekmatyar is closer to Kabul airport than Massoud is. If Hekmatyar captures the airport [which is on the outskirts of the city], he will enter Kabul. And he will plunder it. He is ruthless.

Mr. Sevan must immediately meet with Massoud and with Hekmatyar, and convince them to halt their advances toward Kabul. He must announce his intention to do so before it is too late, even before he can make the necessary arrangements. There must be a declaration by the UN demanding that military action against Kabul cease at once.

Mr. Sevan should meet with General Azimi rather than with Najibullah at this point. General Azimi is in charge of the defense of Kabul. Azimi should make a public declaration that he supports the UN peace process.

I ask if there is any possibility of factional fighting within Kabul.

Yes! the general says. He fears violence from the followers of Karmal, the Khalqi. He has not heard about any deal between the interior minister and Karmal's group. He does not believe there was one.

———

That night, before I go to sleep, I tell Avni to be sure to wake me if there are critical developments. He says he will.

———

16 April 1992

0110 hours. Avni wakes me with a call. Says a car will come to pick me up in fifteen minutes. I have laid my clothes out ahead of time, so that I can leave on short notice. Went to sleep around 11 p.m. When the phone first rings, I am in the middle of a dream. I can't find the telephone. I have forgotten where the lights are. I have forgotten where I am. When I find the phone, I recognize Avni's voice. I splash water on my face to wake up. I check to make sure I have my ID, my notebook, and more than one pen.

———

0130 hours. A UN car arrives. The driver takes me to OSGAP headquarters. From there we leave immediately for Najib's residence. We arrive within minutes. Najib is wearing a dark gray, pinstriped suit, a businessman's attire, and smiling anxiously. He is accompanied by General Toukhi, his chief of staff. Toukhi has his wife and three children (two boys and one girl) with him. Najib is accompanied by his brother, a bodyguard, and a servant. In all, a party of nine, including Najib.

We go inside, and Avni and General Toukhi go to work immediately on the statement by Najib that will formally announce his promised resignation. They have been working on it for the past few days. They are finishing if off now. It will be short.

I sit with Najib while they work. Najib is gracious, effusive. His emotion gushes through his fractured English. Though he is anxious, he seems more beset by sadness than fear. He wants once again to make his case to me. He is sad to leave Afghanistan—the country he has loved, defended; the country of his birth, the country in which his children may never grow up, which he may never see again.

And he is angry. I can feel his anger. It is an earthquake trapped in a jewel box, waiting to erupt. He is being driven out by extremists, barbarians, conspirators, religious fundamentalists. Afghanistan is being betrayed by feudal, medieval warlords in the pay of foreign rulers. The future is being swallowed by the past. He was the keystone that held together the arch that is Afghanistan as the country moved, perhaps too quickly, from feudalism to secular modernism. And now, he fears, the country will retreat into anarchy. It will go backward in time.

He tells me he has told Mr. Sevan many times that he would sacrifice anything, even himself, to bring peace to his country. He knows that the Afghan people want an end to war, but there are certain extremist elements that are against the UN peace plan. He is confident that eventually these elements will be isolated, and Afghanistan will emerge free and independent.

I tell him I hope the UN will be able to prevent any further bloodshed.

He speaks about his children, his wife. They are in New Delhi. He is eager to see them. [I think of my own children, and how much I miss them. But I am certain that I will see them again. What must it be like, I wonder, to fear that you will never again see your children?]

I say I think he is doing the right thing to remove himself from the political process. I hope others will appreciate his gesture.

He says that when he heard I'd arrived in Kabul, he felt good. It was a good sign. He had been waiting to meet me. He stands up and extends his hand to me. I stand up and shake his hand. He embraces me warmly.

[To the Afghan government, as well as to many other international actors in Kabul, my arrival signified that the United States was taking a more active interest in Afghanistan, and specifically, that it supported the UN plan for Afghanistan. The fact that the U.S. Ambassador to Pakistan had already stated his support for the UN plan was a matter of record. But there was still no U.S. Ambassador to Afghanistan, and the fact that a high ranking UN official, who was an American, had arrived in Kabul at this critical juncture was taken to signify an increased interest in Afghanistan on the part of the United States. It was pointless for me to say that I had come as a UN official, and not as a representative of my government. Which was the truth. The Afghans never would have believed it. I'm not even sure Benon and the rest of the UN staff would have believed it. It was simply assumed by members of the international community that every UN official, from whatever country, passed information to his government. Every man/woman in the UN was considered a spy, especially when involved in an event as strategic as war. And of course, some were. For my part, I never wasted my breath on spy talk. I let other people assume what they would.]

Avni comes out from the study where he has been with General Toukhi. He says it is time to leave for the airport. Toukhi will discuss the statement in the car with Najib. Najib has seen the statement earlier. There have not been major changes.

0145 hours. We load the baggage and begin a three-convoy movement to the airport. I am in the front car with Dan Quirke, a UN administrative officer and Irish national. We're in a four-wheel drive, Toyota Land Rover. Quirke is driving. Najib's bodyguard, with a Kalashnikov, is in the back seat with Najib's servant. The second car is a sedan. Avni is driving. Colonel Nowlan is sitting in front, and Najib and his brother are in back in that car. The third vehicle is a Toyota minibus, driven by Major Peter Beier, a UN blue beret from Denmark; with him are General Toukhi and his family.

We pass through several checkpoints, using the code word given to us by the minister of state security that afternoon. Benon has landed the UN plane at Kabul airport. He is inside the plane, waiting for us. [I doubt very much that he has brought with him the fifteen-member Council of Impartials. The original plan was to bring them to Kabul at the same time that Najib was leaving. That way, there would be a transfer of power with no break in the action. But the fact that Benon is arriving in the middle of the night suggests the plan has been abandoned. I have a bad feeling in my nervous stomach.]

When we come to the final checkpoint, we are halted. The guards will not let us pass. The password we have used for the first few checkpoints is suddenly invalid. Quirke tries the password several times, but the guards will not let us through. Then Quirke says a few words in the local language, hoping to convince the guards that everything has been agreed to, that it's all right. He keeps telling them everything is okay. But the guards will not budge. Quirke inches our vehicle forward as he talks. He has a jocular tone to his voice. It is as if he is trying to pull into a parking lot at the beach. Piece of cake. Let us through, he says.

But the guards will not budge. And they are annoyed that Quirke is inching forward. There are three or four of them. One raises his weapon to his shoulder. It is not easy to see them because it is the middle of the night, and the only light is from our headlights. The sky is overcast.

I implore Quirke to stop, to put on the brake. "They're not kidding." I say. "They'd just as soon shoot you as not."

Quirke is one of those fearless Irishmen I have met in peacekeeping operations all over the world. They push up against danger as if it were merely another hill to be climbed, as if all you needed were a little more effort. I was less daring. Quirke stops the car. "They're wearing different uniforms," he says.

"What do you mean?"

"They're wearing different uniforms than the guards at the other checkpoints."

"What does that mean?"

"It means they're special airport guards, or that the airport has changed hands."

"We've been double-crossed," I say.

"Probably," Quirke says.

Najib's bodyguard gets out of our car. He takes his Kalashnikov, but it is slung over his shoulder. He argues with the guards. He shouts at them. Colonel Nowlan gets out of his car, and comes to see what the trouble is. Avni gets out of his car. He wants to listen, not to argue. The shouting continues for about five minutes. I try to watch their gestures, but there is not very much light.

Meanwhile, Avni is in contact with Benon, who is on the UN plane at the airport. They are talking over the mobile phone. They are speaking in Turkish.

Avni comes over to tell us what is happening. The highest-ranking officer at the checkpoint is a sergeant. He has agreed to call his lieutenant to come to the checkpoint to talk to Najib's bodyguard. Dostom's Uzbek troops have seized the airport. They are not letting anyone through. Our password is useless. Perhaps one of the members of the executive committee of the Watan Party, with whom we made our agreement, is a follower of Karmal, Najib's bitter rival and predecessor, and has leaked our plans to Dostom. Or perhaps Dostom merely wants to take over now that Najib has resigned, and he considers Najib to be his prisoner. One should never underestimate the egomaniacal desire for power among certain members of the human species. In any case, Dostom has seized the airport to prevent Najib's escape. He has sealed it off. And apparently, government troops did not put up a fight. As Colonel Nowlan told us recently, the defense perimeter of Kabul is a joke. Dostom's troops will not allow anyone into the airport for twenty-four hours. Meanwhile, Benon cannot disembark. He has ordered the UN plane to be locked, so that no one can board or leave. His plane is surrounded by troops.

A lieutenant arrives within ten minutes, and a bitter argument ensues. There is a lot of shouting. Everyone is calling everyone else names. This is not a negotiation. This is an exchange of threats and insults. We sit and watch. After a while, the officer and Najib's bodyguard go to speak to Najib. According to Avni, Najib is saying something like "Let us through, you asshole! Everything has been arranged!" Najib has a booming voice, even from inside a car. And he knows his life is at stake. After so many years in Afghanistan, after so many deaths behind him, he senses immediately what his fate will be if he can't flee. Death has been his constant companion, even his confidant, for the past decade, perhaps longer.[7] But the lieutenant claims he has no authority to let Najib through, and that even if he could, our whole party would be slaughtered at the airport, because Dostom's troops are not letting anyone in or out of the airport for at least the next 24 hours. Once they have secured the airport, they will allow only certain flights to go in and out. At this point, the Uzbeks will shoot anyone approaching the airport, no questions asked, the lieutenant insists.

After several minutes of shouting, Najib makes a decision. He has very little leverage, he has very few allies, and no longer any power to intimidate or bribe. He tells Avni to turn around. He is convinced they will not be able to reach the airport tonight. Avni asks Najib if he wants to return to his residence. "No!" Najib says. The same forces which have prevented him from leaving Kabul will kill him if he returns to his residence. The only safe place is the OSGAP compound. The UN has an obligation to protect him, he insists.

[It was as if, at this very moment, on this very spot, a power vacuum replaced what little central authority still existed in

Afghanistan; and that is why, I am convinced, this event must be given due significance in any history of this period. On this night, within a few hundred yards of Kabul airport, the sitting president of Afghanistan, Najibullah—a.k.a. Najib-e-Gao, or Najib the Bull—was deposed by anarchy. There had been varying degrees of anarchy in the country for months, but it had never triumphed until that night. Perhaps there would have been anarchy anyway, even if Najib had been able to board the UN plane. Or perhaps his official resignation and sudden exile might have pushed the factions meeting in Peshawar to reach an agreement on the Council of Impartials. We shall never know. But what we do know is that the gods of anarchy, which had been hovering over poor Afghanistan ever since the Soviet Union's withdrawal three years before, descended that night and took control. To be followed within a few years by a murderous medieval gang, swaddled in sanctimony and nurtured in Pakistan, known as the Taliban.]

Avni is still in contact with Benon, keeping him informed of what is happening in the convoy. Benon's plane is surrounded. He cannot move. Benon repeats that he has ordered the plane locked, to discourage the Uzbeks from storming it. But the Uzbeks are armed with grenades. He doubts if they will try to blow up the plane. They know that Najib cannot be on it. They have no reason to blow up the plane. [But less logical things have happened. And logic, which throughout history has frequently deserted Afghanistan, does not have much of a presence at this point.]

At 0200 hours we turn the convoy around and head back to OSGAP headquarters.

[Writing in retrospect, Hassan Kakar gives his own version of events the night before (14 April), which set the stage for what I have just described. Though I have been unable to corroborate Kafar's account, it seems quite credible.

> At 2:00 p.m. on 14 April 1992, the militias of Dostom, which had been brought to Kabul by air, took positions in the city. Surprised, President Najibullah, in a hastily convened session of the Supreme Council of Defense, asked for an explanation. Azimi and other Parchami leaders told him that the militias had been brought to protect Kabul against the threats posed by Hekmatyar, who had concentrated his men at the city's southern limits. They also asked Najibullah to announce this on the mass media and apologize to the nation for having invited the Soviet army in 1979. Giving the impression that he would do so, Najibullah instead went straight to the headquarters of the United Nations; from there he asked Benon Sevan, who was in Islamabad at the time, to come immediately to Kabul. After Sevan arrived, Najibullah arranged to fly with him abroad, but Dostom's militia controlled the airport and refused to let him go.[8]]

As we turned our convoy around that night I was immediately aware that the events surrounding Najib's aborted escape from Kabul had a significance that went far beyond the borders of Afghanistan, and related to UN peacekeeping operations in general. Our drama had been played out many times in the past, in the most remote corners of the globe, and would no doubt occur again. The fact was, we had just been threatened by men with guns. Benon was still trapped and a virtual hostage. In a sense we were all hostages, albeit to a lesser degree. Indeed, the number of life-threatening situations UN personnel (civilians as well as soldiers) face during a peacekeeping operation is one of the many facts unknown and unappreciated by the general public, certainly by the American public. While it is true that soldiers are trained for such situations, and that UN civilian officials have volunteered for such missions with full awareness of the potential dangers, the face of death is always frightening and ugly when it appears, no matter what the verbal preparation. The Nobel Prize Committee recognized the courage of the Blue Helmets (UN peacekeeping forces) when it awarded them the Nobel Peace Prize in 1988. But UN civilian officials, with the exception of the secretary-general, are yet to receive much recognition or appreciation for their efforts, even though, from the heads of mission down to the lowest-ranking election monitor or jeep driver, they often put their lives at risk in the service of the international community. The Western public frequently hears tales (real or imagined) about corruption, bloated budgets, and freeloading by UN personnel. But the mortal dangers they face, as well as their numerous achievements, are conveniently ignored. I am not suggesting that UN civilian personnel in the field should be sanctified, or idealized like matinee idols in a soap opera. But what they do merit is more respect that they are getting, especially from the Great Deadbeat in Washington, which refuses to pay its dues, often refuses to participate in UN ground operations, and condescendingly skewers UN peacekeeping operations at every opportunity. How I wished at that very moment in the middle of the night in Kabul, with several teenage boys pointing weapons at us, that I might have had a few influential members of the U.S. Congress with me in the convoy. Preferably in the front car, where I was sitting.

[Looking back, it was clear we had no idea that General Dostom would seize the airport that night. As I noted briefly in my preface, Gianni Picco reports a conversation he had with Benon earlier that day in which Picco expressed his concern about whether anyone would fill the power vacuum in Kabul once Najib left. Picco was very well informed about Afghanistan. He had been involved in the negotiations that, in 1988, finally brought about a complete withdrawal of the Soviet Union's troops from Afghanistan. It was one of the UN's finest hours, and had been led by the diplomatic efforts of a brilliant, sharp-tongued UN diplomat from Ecuador, Diego Cordovez, who later went on to become his country's foreign minister. But Picco, for all his good contacts, had no advance knowledge of Dostom's imminent power play.

Najib was an albatross around our necks, but we could not abandon him. I remembered once having had a discussion with James O. Jonah, a former boss of mine and an under secretary-general for political affairs, after I had returned from Afghanistan. How could the UN feel a moral obligation to Najibullah? I asked him. Najibullah had probably been responsible for the deaths of thousands of his countrymen. Jonah, a tall and imposing African from Sierra Leone, holder of a Ph.D. in political science from MIT, patiently made the distinction for me between a political and moral obligation. The UN had never endorsed Najib's policies, he noted. The UN was trying to bring peace, stability and self-government to Afghanistan, in accordance with the good offices of the secretary-general. Guaranteeing safe passage to Najib in exchange for his resignation had been part of that effort.]

0220 hours. We arrive at the OSGAP compound. Avni is still speaking to Benon on the mobile radio. They are in constant contact. They are speaking Turkish. Benon knows about our having been turned back. He knows we are bringing Najib to OSGAP headquarters.

We arrive back at the UN compound. Najib and General Toukhi go first to Avni's office, then to Benon's office. Their luggage remains in the vehicles. [Avni told me later that Najib had wanted to call his wife in New Delhi to tell her his escape had been blocked, but Avni insisted that Najib first call one or two generals who were still loyal to him in order to release Benon, who was locked in his plane, and in mortal danger.]

———

0245 hours. Benon calls from the airport to say he is still on the plane, and the plane cannot leave. It is surrounded by Uzbek soldiers. He can see them from the plane.

———

0250 hours. Benon calls again. Three generals have arrived at the airport, in Mercedes, apparently in response to Najib's summons. Benon sees them. He recognizes Generals Azimi and Delawar. They are negotiating with the militia at the airport. The generals know their best hope for survival is with the UN. They need Benon alive.

Najib has also spoken briefly to the minister of state security [i.e., head of the secret police], Ghulam Faruq Yaqoubi, demanding an explanation. Yaqoubi said he would call back. [He never did. The next day it was reported that Yaqoubi had committed suicide. Afghan contacts said he had been murdered. Who knows? Perhaps Yaqoubi knew he was doomed and chose a more desirable alternative. Or perhaps an ambitious subordinate murdered him in order to claim a trophy and save his own neck. Either way, death was to have its tribute.]

0300 hours. Benon and Andrew Gilmore (Benon's personal assistant) are allowed to disembark. They will come to the OSGAP compound immediately. Meanwhile, the UN plane remains on the ground, surrounded by troops. I am sitting in Benon's office, with Najib and General Toukhi. Najib says to me, in his fractured English: "You see? These are the *extreme elements* I was talking about. And this is only the beginning." [Najib sees himself as a moderate between the old feudal regime and the new fundamentalists.]

─────────

0315 hours. The UN pilot calls on our mobile phone to say he will be allowed to leave. We tell him to notify us once he is airborne. [In effect, we have conceded that Najib will not be able to board the plane with him tonight.] Within minutes the plane departs successfully. We are in the UN compound with our cargo.

─────────

0320 hours. Benon arrives from the airport with General Azimi. Avni has already contacted the Indian Embassy to ask for political asylum for Najibullah. We estimate that we have a couple of hours until daylight, at which time local workers will be arriving at the compound. By then, the entire town, the entire world, will know what has happened.

─────────

0400 hours. Benon calls the director-general of the Pakistan embassy to ask him to clear a plan with mujahidin leaders in Peshawar. Under this plan, in exchange for safe passage for Najib, a military council would immediately take charge in Kabul, headed by General Azimi. The Council of Impartials could then take over from the military council. Benon wants to see a peaceful transfer of power, as took place recently in cities to the north. He reads to the director-general the names that would be on the military council.

———

0420 hours. The idea of a military council is collapsing. Benon has spoken to Azimi again. The names on Azimi's list are not available any longer. Several of them are trying to make their own deals, or have fled.

———

0430 hours. Benon calls Gianni Picco in New York, and informs him what has transpired. Benon expresses his concern that there might be an attack on UN premises. "The luggage was never delivered," he says, speaking in an improvised code. "We have a time bomb here. These guys are butchers."

[That morning at UN headquarters in New York, Secretary-General Boutros-Ghali issued a statement expressing his disturbance with "the news he has received from his Personal Representative in Kabul concerning the development that took place in the night of 15 to 16 April." He added that he expected that "the safety of all United Nations personnel would be respected and that they would be allowed freedom of movement in and out of the country as their responsibilities require."]

———

0435 hours. The Indian chargé d'affaires arrives to say he thinks he can give asylum to Najib at the Indian embassy in Kabul, but he has to have an official request from Benon, and he has to clear it with New Delhi. Avni departs to draft a *note verbale* to the Indian Chargé.

0515 hours. The Indian ambassador brings us bad news. New Delhi is worried about possible reprisals against the Indian community in Kabul if India grants asylum to Najib. Therefore, he is reluctant to grant asylum to Najib.

———

0530 hours. Benon decides to contact several other ambassadors in order to discuss alternatives. We live in fear of the dawn, when the city will awake to the news of what has happened. We assume that Watan Party officials, who control the local media, have already informed them about Najib's aborted attempt to escape. Also, at dawn many of the townspeople go to their local mosque, where they pray and exchange information. Mosques have a social as well as a political function, especially in times of great crisis.

———

0615 hours. We are all high on adrenaline. Nobody is sleepy. Delegations from India, Turkey, Iran, France, Pakistan, China, and Italy arrive. Benon is on the phone in the other room. They ask me why they have been summoned. I tell them that Benon will inform them in a few moments, but they are insistent on being informed immediately. They have been awakened early in the morning and demand an explanation. I inform them our attempt to evacuate Najib has failed, and that he is here at the OSGAP compound. They gasp.

Benon arrives and addresses the delegations. He says he had intended to fly to India with Najib, but when the UN plane landed, it was surrounded. He had not expected that sort of reception. Not a single person at the airport spoke English, and there were no interpreters. He and his entire party had been virtual prisoners. Finally, General Azimi had showed up, and Benon had offered to stay behind in

Kabul if the UN plane were allowed to take off. He had been concerned about the safety of the air crew, and he realized he would not be able to evacuate Najib tonight. The troops at the airport, with General Azimi's help, had agreed, and the UN plane had been able to return to Pakistan.

0645 hours. Pakistan agrees to offer asylum to Najib at the Pakistan Embassy in Kabul. We arrange for an armored van to be ready to transport Najib and his party from the OSGAP compound to the Pakistan embassy. We are hopeful. The transfer could be accomplished in minutes and would take effect before the city awoke.

0655 hours. Benon presents Pakistan's offer to Najib. Present in Benon's office, in addition to Avni, Benon, and me, are the representatives of Pakistan and Iran. Avni acts as interpreter.

Najib's performance runs a gamut of emotions. At first, he speaks in a firm but subdued voice, carefully gauging his audience, offering political analyses and speaking with dignity as a chief of state, visibly restraining his emotion, portraying himself and his country as victims of forces beyond their control, perhaps even as victims of an international plot. But within minutes his restraint evaporates, and his anger rises like yeast. He is a cornered beast in the body of a man, torn between the conflicting loyalties of honor and patriotism on the one hand and the most primal instinct to save his life and see his family again on the other.

Najib: I said I would submit my resignation in pursuit of the UN peace plan if it would help to end hostilities, and if there would be no assault on Kabul. I warned you that if I announced my intention to resign before an interim gov-

ernment was in place that there would be a power vacuum. This is what is happening today. I fought these developments for three years; I knew what would happen. Once
a power vacuum emerges, who will be responsible for law
and order and security? Not only the honor and pride of
Najibullah are at stake, but also the honor and pride of the
UN. I WILL NOT GO TO PAKISTAN! That is no solution.
I prefer to stay at the UN compound. The answer is the UN
peace plan, and the Council of Impartials, which will take
over as a transitional authority as soon as possible.

As Najib speaks, he shakes his finger at Benon and at
the representatives of Iran and Pakistan, accusing them of
betraying their promises and provoking ethnic conflict
inside Afghanistan. [At this point Najib's sense of national
pride and his political instincts, his Marxist training, have
overtaken his anxieties about survival. He feels he is safe
within the UN compound, and he refuses to accept asylum
from the very countries that he believes have intervened in
Afghanistan and provoked violence. His hatred for the representatives of Pakistan and Iran is palpable. It hangs in the
air like an acid cloud.]

The Iranian representative, responding to Najib's concern that there will be an assault on Kabul now that he has
resigned, says that Iran will make every effort to restrain
mujahidin elements from attacking the capital. He regrets
the verbal attacks against his country by President Najibullah. Iran has provided asylum for two million Afghan
refugees. Iran is a friendly neighbor.

Benon (to Najib): I don't know if I can provide you with
proper protection here. You would be safer at an embassy.
[Benon would like Najib out of UN premises as soon as pos-
sible. If not, he fears, as he told Picco when he called New
York, that there may be an assault on the UN compound.
Such an attack would endanger UN personnel, embarrass

the UN, and unquestionably put Najib's life in danger. Moreover, to keep Najib at the UN compound compromises the UN's negotiating position. It makes the UN a part of the problem rather than a part of the solution. We become Najib's protectors. We are seen as protecting not only his person but also his political views.]

Najib (to all): Guarantees given by the mujahidin and their sponsors (i.e., Pakistan and Iran) are useless. In the north, mujahidin commanders have sworn they would brutally destroy the Kabul regime. They say that the proposed Council of Impartials is composed of pro-Westerners and supporters of the former King. They always have excuses for not agreeing to the UN plan. I want implementation of the UN plan. Mr. Sevan is a witness to what I said earlier. I said that once the transfer of power had begun, I would resign. But he said *no*, that I should resign before. I warned there would be a power vacuum if I resigned before the Council of Impartials was in place. That has, in effect, happened. The intent of recent actions is to destroy the UN plan. The mujahidin are claiming that the UN Plan is pro-Western or pro-Royalist. That is nonsense. I myself set no conditions regarding the list of Impartials. The UN should pressure all sides to agree to the UN plan. Unless the UN plan is adopted, the north will be split off and Afghanistan will be partitioned.

In very strong language and gestures, Najib then denounces Pakistan and Iran, saving his most bitter barbs for Iran. Though this is certainly not a comic situation, Najib at this moment reminds me of the comic strip hero, the Incredible Hulk; he seems to enlarge with each phrase, puff up like a venomous adder, as though he were about to explode out of his skin.

Najib: Each day Pakistan says it wants no clashes, yet it

continues to support the mujahidin. And Iran also supports the muj, no matter what it says!

Najib is screaming at the Iranian delegate, who is a short, slight man. At one point, I fear Najib, with his massive hands, will simply walk over and pick the man up and throw him out the nearest window. [Perhaps he would have if we were not there.]

Najib (facing Benon): "I offered my resignation today as president of the Republic of Afghanistan, and as leader of the ruling Watan Party. The UN now has the responsibility to make its plan work. I am prepared to sacrifice myself if anyone tries to attack the UN premises, if that will help to bring peace to my country. I am willing to make the *ultimate* sacrifice."

The discussion continues for several minutes, but it is more of the same. Offers for asylum are made and rejected. There are denunciations, accusations, and somber predictions. Najib does most of the talking. He hates, despises, and verbally abuses the Iranian and Pakistani representatives. He clutches at the UN like a drowning man at a life preserver, even though he knows, he must know, that the UN is powerless at this point, perhaps even discredited. [If the fighting factions do not want a Council of Impartials there will be none. It is that simple. In a country of fierce warriors, where tradition dictates that military victory always takes precedence over diplomacy, there is no likelihood that the UN can impose a peace of any kind, even by appointing a "pre-interim" Council of Impartials.]

Benon and Avni leave. The ambassadors leave with them. I am left alone with Najib and his bodyguard. I am terribly fascinated by Najib. For, whatever else I think of him, I must admire his furious expression of political independence. *I don't trust you, you bastards!* he is saying to

Iran and Pakistan. *I would rather die than be protected by you. And besides, I don't believe you will protect me.*

Najib turns to me and again bitterly denounces "the fundamentalists." He sees them as his main enemy. He never mentions the fact that Washington has armed and supported them as a force to combat the Soviet Union. He makes no reference to the fact that the Soviet Union has deserted him. He is not interested in geopolitics. He is not interested in Big Power politics. He sees the fundamentalists as the main threat to the stability of the region. They are causing problems in North Africa, in Lebanon, in India, in Kashmir. They are the enemies of peace, and they must be stopped. The first place to stop them is here in Afghanistan.

I tell him I agree with him, which I do. I also believe that fundamentalism is the main threat to stability in the world. The Cold War is over. Communism is no longer a serious threat.

I listen to Najib fulminate for several minutes. One of the strongest weapons in a negotiator's arsenal is the ability to listen. Not passively, but actively. To concentrate on what his interlocutor is saying. That is how one gains the confidence of others.

After some minutes I excuse myself. I tell Najib I will return. He rises to shake my hand. He tells me he trusts the UN.

[One final note, for the record. Benon later informed me that he had intended to ask several delegates to accompany him in a convoy to bring Najib to the airport. That would have given Najib more protection and added authority to the UN action. But Benon had arrived too late. He had been negotiating with the various mujahidin groups in Peshawar in a valiant but vain attempt to get agreement on a list of Impartials. Had Benon arrived a day earlier, or even hours earlier, perhaps Najib might have been able to leave. But how could Benon have known the Uzbeks would take over the airport? And how could he have abandoned the negotiations in Peshawar so long as there was hope they might succeed? Benon's critics have suggested that there was never any hope of reaching compromise with the "Peshawar Seven," as they were called, and that Najib's resignation was premature. But such hindsight is self-serving. Perhaps the only point of unity among the various guerrilla factions was the demand for Najib to relinquish power. It was the centerpiece for the negotiating table. How could it be ignored?]

1330 hours. Benon and I go to Watan Party headquarters for a meeting with the Party's executive committee. I have managed to steal about two hours of sleep this morning. I don't think Benon has slept since he left Peshawar yesterday.

Our interlocutor is Sulaiman Layeq.

Layeq: You have asked us in the past if we would be prepared to transfer power, through the UN, to an interim authority. We agreed. We accepted the UN peace plan. The UN is free to set up a Council of Impartials; the number of people on the Council is unimportant. The Council can then act as an authority until an interim government takes power.

Sevan: I told you that if civilian authority didn't pass to this Council, the peace plan wouldn't work. There must be a Council.

Layeq: Yes, but if only civilian authority is transferred, there will be dual forces. There is a need to transfer military power also. Civilian authority is not enough. We could form a Council of Commanders, if you wish, to prepare for a transfer of military authority.

Sevan: Yes, that is a possibility.

Layeq: We will prepare the names.

Sevan: Do you foresee a deal in Kabul as in Mazir-i-Sharif? Can we avoid bloodshed?

Layeq: That is unpredictable. No one could have predicted the resignation of the president. Or other developments.

Sevan: Would you accept a Council of Impartials without Watan Party representation?

Layeq: What is the point of disarming our party? It would cause havoc.

Sevan: It might make it easier to end hostilities. [We all know that the mujahidin want no communists on the Council. And we also know that the Watan Party has precious little, if any, leverage at this point. The victors in this war will have no magnanimity. In fact, while Benon is trying to think of ways to mitigate the impending doom, Layeq is trying to save his own life. The talk about "Party" is a ruse. The scenario is Alice in Hades. "Disarming" the Watan Party is like defanging a dead snake.]

Layeq: It would cause anarchy.

Sevan: I have just now received a message from Pakistan. The news is encouraging. They believe they have ten names agreed upon for the Council of Impartials. If these people arrive in Kabul, would your ministers be willing to resign?

Layeq: Yes, of course. (The others at the conference table nod in agreement.) That is what must happen. The Council should have authority to make decisions from now on. It would stabilize the situation.

Sevan: Good. Then we are agreed on that. Now, there is still the question of Najibullah. As you know, he has been a major obstacle in all peace talks. For a long time I have been making a major effort to overcome this obstacle. It has not been easy. But finally, on 18 March, I convinced Najibullah to make a statement that he would be willing to step down and not participate in the Council of Impartials or in the interim government. Although the formal resignation of Najibullah had been sought by all factions, we were aware that it was necessary to avoid a power vacuum once he resigned. The continued presence of President Najibullah in Kabul would not be beneficial to the peace process, because opponents would insist he was meddling in politics even if he were out of office. Therefore, it was essential that he be taken out of the country *immediately and safely*. If anything were to happen to him, it would reflect unfavorably on Afghanistan. He must be guaranteed safe passage out of the country if the peace process is to succeed.

Layeq: What happened last night when you tried to fly Najibullah out of the country was unfortunate, particularly because he was able to involve the UN. The action Najibullah took, to try to leave the country like a thief in the night, was regrettable, because he did not consult either with the party or the state, and he even endangered your life. He should be transferred to his house. We will guarantee his safety and health there, until we decide where he will be allowed to go.

Sevan: You are putting the UN in a difficult position. Najibullah has sought refuge at the UN. If we turn him away it will be bad for the peace process. We must resolve this problem, or it will become a major international incident with consequences no one can predict. Besides, how can I persuade members of the Council of Impartials to come to a place where security will be guaranteed, if I cannot guarantee the safety of President Najibullah? The only reason the UN became involved in this problem was because it wanted to remove an obstacle to peace. If this issue is not resolved immediately, there can be no solution to larger problems. You must decide which is more important for you: to prevent President Najibullah from leaving Kabul, or to go ahead with the peace process. It is your decision.

Layeq: We should have discussed Najibullah before this situation developed.

Sevan: We had an agreement. We were promised safe passage. Why didn't you let our convoy through the checkpoint?

Layeq: There are certain procedures we must pursue in all cases, not only in yours.

Sevan: But we had an agreement.

Layeq: There was a misunderstanding. As I said, there are certain procedures that apply in *all* cases. [Though Benon is acting as if it were Layeq who gave the order to stop our convoy before it reached the airport, it was not clear who had actually blocked us last night. Probably it had been Dostom's men who had prevented us from evacuating Najib, but Benon wasn't sure, and it was the Watan Party with whom Benon had made the agreement, not Dostom. I recalled Dan Quirke's observation that the uniforms of the soldiers at the final checkpoint were different from those of the soldiers at earlier checkpoints. I suspected that Layeq was only pretending to have had a hand in the act in order to enhance his own and his party's prestige, to aspire to authority he didn't have. He wanted to share in the credit for having prevented Najib from leaving the country now that Najib was out of power and regarded as a criminal.]

Sevan: So, what will we do about Najibullah? [Benon was trying to gather information. How long would the airport be closed? Who was holding it? We, too, were growing desperate. Desperate to get Najib off of our hands. We were on a fishing expedition. We were unarmed lifeguards swimming in a sea of sharks.]

Layeq: Najibullah may stay with you, but he should not be allowed to leave the premises of the UN compound until a decision is made as to where he will go. Don't you, Mr. Sevan, feel safe when you are in Afghanistan? That proves we can guarantee safety.

Sevan: I do not come to Afghanistan because I feel safe, but because I love your country. However, I must remind you that my office has been hit by rockets, and my plane has seventy-two bullet holes.

Layeq: You have accepted great risks, it is true, but you have earned great prestige and respect for the United Nations. In any case, the attacks on your plane and your office were not by our forces. We respect the UN and would never fire on it.

Sevan: The main concern now is how to bring peace to this country. You will achieve nothing by making Najibullah remain in Kabul. It will only obstruct the peace process. On another matter, I hope that since you are in charge of security, you can assure me there will be no mass demonstrations in front of the OSGAP compound. If there is an invasion of UN premises, it would create a major embarrassment for all. We cannot let emotions take over at a time like this. You must understand that when the president of a country asks for my help, I feel obligated to honor my pledge. Since President Najibullah offered to resign and asked to leave the country, I took it for granted that he had consulted with you. I hope you will understand my position. Now, what about preventing mass demonstrations?

Layeq: You can be assured that there will be no demonstrations in front of the UN premises. But we request you not to move Najibullah from the OSGAP compound until we say so.

Sevan: I cannot leave Kabul until this issue is resolved. I am supposed to go to Mazar-i-Sharif today, but I will not go until this issue is resolved, and I hope they do not interpret it there as being a snub to them. One more thought about Najibullah. Because many groups and individuals may want to reach him, you are encouraging belligerent actions within Kabul by not letting him leave.

[At this point Benon hands to the executive committee Najibullah's official letter of resignation. It is read out loud.]

Layeq: We do not recognize the validity of this letter. We will not announce it on state radio.

Sevan: The UN will not announce it either. But the international media have a copy of it. They will announce it.

Layeq: The people in Kabul are calm. The announcement will not upset them. Meanwhile, you can feel safe in Kabul. The security around the city is good. Oh, yes, by the way. General Yaqoubi, the minister for state security, has committed suicide. There will be a funeral for him tomorrow. (I immediately doubted it was suicide.)

Sevan: Let's try to meet again tomorrow at 9 a.m.

Layeq: Of course.

---

17 April 1992

1100 hours. Turkish embassy. Briefing by Benon. Agenda item: Preparations for security in case of need for quick evacuation. The UN has 91 non-OSGAP personnel, including 14 in Mazar-i-Sharif. The 91 personnel are mostly humanitarian aid workers. OSGAP itself has 14 persons. Total, 105 UN personnel. (Imagine! *Fourteen* persons trying to prevent a calamity of massive proportion, trying to pacify thousands of armed soldiers. Is this courage or absurdity?)

Benon begins his briefing by saying that the resignation of Najibullah yesterday was completely in line with the

President Najibullah displays a copy of the Koran with bullet holes through it during a news conference in Kabul, on 20 January 1987. He said the hole had been made by a mujahidin bullet. (Associated Press Photo/Andrew Rosenthal)

Najibullah, left, with his brother, Shahpur Ahmedzi, center, 27 September 1996, hanged by Taliban forces in front of the presidential palace in Kabul. The two men had been sequestered in the UN compound since 16 April 1992. (Associated Press Photo/Hader Shah)

Uzbek warlord Abdul Rashid Dostom in Mazar-i-Sharif. Dostom's forces seized Kabul airport in April 1992 and prevented Najibullah's escape. (Associated Press Photo/B. K. Bangash)

Soldiers loyal to Uzbek warlord Abdul Rashid Dostom. (Associated Press/ Arthur Max)

announcement of 18 March that he would resign. It was totally consistent with the UN peace plan. There had been an understanding among all parties that it would be best if Najib resigned and left the country. His resignation was intended to bring unity to the country. This was not an unusual scenario. A coalition was expected to replace him, and to begin the process of healing. But those who had guaranteed his departure had changed their minds at the very last minute and undermined the procedure. Now, even though the Afghan government wanted Najib, Benon had told them categorically that Najib had sought refuge at the UN, and the UN would provide him protection. If any attempt were made to storm the UN premises, it would create an ugly international incident and obstruct the peace process. The UN had requested that Najib be given safe passage out of the country to a place where he could be granted political asylum. Benon had requested several governments to make démarches to the Afghan government, asking safe passage for Najib. Until this issue was resolved, the peace process was stalled, and Benon would not leave Afghanistan. He was still hoping for a Council of Impartials to be appointed.

In response to a question, Benon acknowledged that the definition of "impartial" was still open to discussion. But definitions were not the problem, as we all knew. The problems were treachery, revenge, and a struggle for power. The issue was who would control the lucrative drug trade.

The Turkish chargé then read out a brief English-language summary of a statement made by Abdul Wakil, the Afghan foreign minister, on radio last night. Wakil said that former President Najibullah had tried to escape but had been stopped by the armed forces. (*Whose* armed forces? I wondered.) He must be held to answer certain questions to the Afghan people. The government had no intention of killing him. The soldiers at the checkpoint could have killed him, but did not. Wakil said the Afghan government still supported the UN peace process. The Afghan government wanted to have the pretransition Council of Impartials in place as soon as possible. An attempt was being made by the Afghan government to form a military council to take control of Kabul until a pretransition Council could be put in place.

The meeting then forms a committee, made up of China, Italy, Pakistan, India, Russia, Iran, and UNDP, to examine emergency evacuation procedures. Another meeting is scheduled for tomorrow.

———

18 April 1992

0600 hours. Benon insisted yesterday that I move my effects into the OSGAP compound. He wants all

OSGAP personnel in the compound. So, I slept at the compound last night in a tiny, monkish cell, with no furniture, shades, or heater. It was cold, but I slept well anyhow. Sandbags stacked high by the window, very little light. Toilet and shower across the narrow corridor. No towels. Must return to my apartment sometime today to pick up my laundry and a few towels. The room here reminds me of the one where I once slept in Tindouf, Algeria, while on a peacekeeping mission in Western Sahara. But it was warmer in the desert. And because the base there was being used by a unit of the French army, they had a pastry chef who prepared wonderful treats every afternoon at 4 p.m. A major morale booster, that was. And then the stars. In the desert there is no smog, and so the stars are incredibly bright, as if someone had cleaned and polished the lenses in your eyes. It is awesome, majestic.

[Laundry. One day someone will write a memoir about the role of laundry in revolutionary situations. You never know where it is. Often in three or four different places at the same time. You move, leave your effects behind. We should have throw-away laundry. As for soldiers at war, they don't have time to do their laundry. They simply sweat and stink.

Although all facts seem to suggest that we are living on the edge of potential destruction, I still cannot believe I am in mortal danger. Perhaps I'm in a state of denial. I just cannot imagine being killed, throat cut, blown up by a rocket lobbed into the compound, shot by a firing squad, executed for being a spy, etc. Or being captured and imprisoned and tortured. Or stepping on a land mine. Those are all abstract, intellectual concepts. None of them grabs me by the throat, knocks me to my knees directly, forces me into prayer, or makes me reconsider my last will and testament. Of course, it is not unusual to deny death. And doing so is not necessarily an act of courage. I recall Ernest Becker's classic work, *The Denial of Death*. Becker believed the main motivation of mankind was to deny death, and that was why he constructed so many systems, ideas, structures, illusions, etc....Is that why I am thinking about laundry?]

Avni and Andrew have already moved into the compound. Benon is in a "siege" mentality. Until yesterday, I was staying in the house that Benon rents, about ten minutes walking distance from the compound. It is a large house, has several bedrooms. Benon is concerned about my safety. He fears the mujahidin may come looking for him in the middle of the night. If they break into the house and I am there, I may be endangered, taken hostage, killed. He worries that the mujahidin may be angry with the UN, and with him personally, because they think he is protecting Najibullah. I tell him I am unafraid, and that it is more comfortable to sleep in the house. If I have a mobile radio, I can call if help is needed. But Benon is insistent, and so I move into the compound.

Half an hour ago, at 0530 hours, the BBC reported forty thousand troops had massed north of Kabul: Massoud's men. (I suspect this figure is inflated.) The BBC also reported twenty thousand troops south of the city, loyal to Hekmatyar. It is uncertain at this point if General Dostom still controls Kabul airport. Probably he does, but no one can get close enough to find out for sure. We are trapped. At least, we are grounded. We cannot fly out. A UN plane coming from Pakistan would probably be unable to land; if it did, it might not be able to take off. And if it could take off, it might be shot down once it was airborne by stinger missiles (originally provided by Washington to the mujahidin who now surround the airport, thank you). The air route from Kabul to Islamabad must go south, over territory controlled by Hekmatyar, and the mujahidin might think the UN plane was carrying Najibullah. Ground transportation is not safe either. Even the main roads may be mined. We do not know.

[Hekmatyar hates Benon and the UN, because he feels that Benon, by protecting Najib, is protecting a Marxist government in Kabul. Hekmatyar, a former professor of religion, is an Islamist. He is fiercely anticommunist, anti-secular. He wants none of the UN peace plan, never has. He is generally believed to be ruthless, vengeful.]

The Indian chargé arrives. He is talking to Benon. Benon is wearing a dark suit, without a tie. He is unshaven, chain-smoking, anxious. He is like a character in an Ionesco play. The world around him is falling apart, and he is trying to make sense of it; he is, in the view of Najib's detractors, trying to climb out of the pit that is Afghanistan, and the sides are all scree. He is trying to save the life of a murderer—whom he has convinced to resign his murderous position—in order to save the life of a country. He is trying to act honorably to save a dishonorable man.

[This is not to say that Benon's actions are absurd. It is the situation that is absurd, and at the same time, painfully real. Benon is trying to act rationally in a situation that is absurd. And inevitably, for all his caution, for all his realistic paranoia, he has been undercut by the very leaders he was trying to assist. He had no choice but to trust them, and they have betrayed him. And in a sense, to the extent that they have undermined the peace process, they have betrayed themselves.]

The UN appears to have the support of the Afghan government, such as it is. No doubt that is because the Watan Party is so weak that it looks to the UN to protect it. At the same time, the Afghan government is hedging its bets. Najib is a new chip, and perhaps he may be a better bargaining chip than the UN's political efforts. The Afghan leaders are terrified, and they are searching for bargaining chips, for leverage. Twenty-four hours ago, the chip named Najibullah was not available. He was one of them, one of those now grasping. Now he is a blue chip, a potential hostage to exchange for their survival. They would love to have him. They would love to be able to auction him off. That was what was behind their offer to "protect" him.

Still, aside from Najib, there is a split with the Watan Party on other issues: the extent of their participation in the new Council, amnesty for political criminals, who will control the military, and so on. Benon cannot depend on a unified party. At this crucial moment when each individual in the collapsing government is looking for a way to survive, there is no one to trust. Not a single piece of shipwreck will float. Any agreement Benon gets may be undermined by a telephone call as soon as he leaves the room.]

1800 hours. At the Iranian mission. Meeting of all missions in Kabul to discuss security arrangements. About thirty missions are represented. Benon stresses that it is important for all concerned to think of this as an Afghan issue, not as an ethnic issue. He appeals for démarches to the Afghan government from as many countries as possible to guarantee safe passage for Najib to leave the country. Several governments agree to make the effort. Though the Afghan government is virtually defenseless against external attack, it still has the power to block Najib's escape—or, at least, his route to the airport. Once at the airport, there may be further problems, depending upon who controls the airport at that moment, and we must anticipate those problems. Therefore, we must also approach the mujahidin. Dostom's forces may still be controlling the airport, and the plane will have to fly over territory controlled by Hekmatyar. We must have the agreement of the muj, as well as of the Afghan government, if Najib is to be flown safely out of Afghanistan.

[The strategy seems to be developing along these lines: Pakistan and Iran will appeal to the muj, while France and Turkey and others will appeal to the Afghan government. Of course, even if agreements are made, it is not certain they will be carried out. There is no such possibility as an agreement in principle, because none of the players has any principle, and no single faction trusts any other faction. And very few of the governments who support the UN peace process trust each other. Finally, because of its involvement in Najibullah's attempted escape, and because it is providing asylum for Najibullah, the UN itself has become a part of the problem rather than a part of the solution. This is the ultimate nightmare for every UN mission, that it should become an issue in and of itself. Seen as the protector of Najibullah, the UN has lost credibility with those whose cooperation it needs most.

Perhaps, if we had been able to evacuate Najib safely out of the country, the various muj factions might no longer have been able to postpone putting an interim civilian authority in place. However, the *manner* in which Najib left office influenced the entire peace process. His failed escape turned the UN into an accessory after the fact, and weakened its position as an interlocutor. The Islamic prosecutors were suddenly strengthened in the court of public opinion, and defense counsel was compromised.

The power vacuum has suddenly become a new ingredient in the mix, perhaps the most powerful ingredient of all. There are those who will say a power vacuum was inevitable, that it had been gaining strength for months, ever since Najibullah announced his intention to resign. But such retrospective clairvoyance is not verifiable. The fact was that Najib as president was a very different commodity than Najib as hostage. A theoretical power vacuum is different than an actual one.]

————

1930 hours. Office of Foreign Minister Wakil. The representatives of India, Pakistan, Russia, and Iran are present. Their presence shows support for the UN plan, and solidarity on the question of allowing Najibullah to leave the country.

Benon (to Wakil): On behalf of the UN secretary-general, I appeal to your government on humanitarian grounds to help insure the safe departure of the former president and his entourage out of Afghanistan. I believe this would help your government at the international level, and help the peace process. This is an urgent matter.

Wakil: It is not too late for a peaceful settlement. But had this request for assistance from our government been expressed earlier, in consultation, there would have been a simple resolution to the problem. There is an Afghan proverb: *Let it be late, but let it be sweet.* We agree that Najibullah had been regarded by all sides as a major obstacle to peace. Our hope was that his departure, along with other officials, would be done in a calm and peaceful manner. Until his very last days in office, Najib had said he would not allow any power vacuum to develop. He wanted a peaceful transition of power. Then suddenly, without pressure from the government, or the party, or the people, he placed everyone in a difficult position, including the UN, by the manner in which he chose to act. This was shameful.

In previous talks with the UN, I had expressed the wish that Najib be returned to his residence. He would be safe there. Why did he decide to create a power vacuum, and cause panic? Would you allow me to leave my job suddenly if it were to create a power vacuum? Why else would General Yaqoubi have committed suicide except for the pressure created by Najib's actions? [Each time I heard that General Yaqoubi had committed suicide, I became more convinced that he had been executed.]

Is the UN concerned for the welfare of only one person? Shouldn't it be concerned for all government members? For the entire country? Everyone should benefit from the efforts of the UN. Nobody in the entire state of Afghanistan expected this act. Never before in the history of Afghanistan has this been done. A president runs away without the slightest consultation! Why was there no consultation with the government, or with the armed forces? Nevertheless, we want to cooperate fully with the UN.

The fact that the representatives of India and the Russian Federation have come to plead for Najib is not surprising, since they were his old friends and supporters. As for Pakistan and Iran, they were always accusing Najib of being an infidel, a Soviet puppet. Now, they are suddenly asking humanitarian consideration for him.

How can we convince the people we are doing right if we let Najib leave? The Afghan population will question us, in light of the fact that Najibullah has committed an illegal act. We must inform the Afghan people of our meeting here tonight. We must let them know of the international appeals on behalf of Najibullah. I will convey your appeal, through the media, to the people. We shall seek their response, and then consider a proper course of action, consistent with the national interest.

Sevan: I am concerned about your going to the media. That might cause hysteria.

Wakil: We would only be helping your cause by letting the people know that it is not only a few people who are making this appeal, but that the appeal comes from very important governments as well. The people should know, for example, that Pakistan and Iran support this appeal.

Sevan: I would prefer to handle this matter privately, not to have it publicized.

Wakil: The press knows we are meeting. I have to tell them something. If you wish, I can say that we met to discuss implementation of the UN peace process.

Sevan: That would be preferable.

Wakil: But I would still like to remind you that if you had consulted with us, we would have agreed to allow Najib to leave peacefully.

Sevan: We had assumed he had consulted with you. We had no time to be concerned with details. That was his responsibility.

Wakil: Have you any idea how much gold Najibullah has smuggled out of our country? He cannot leave with so much gold.

Sevan: I have no idea about such things. I am only interested in promoting the peace process.

———————

2230 hours. I go to see Najib and General Toukhi. They are installed in the upper floor of the far building, which used to house our offices and the briefing room. Najib is in a blue suit, eyes slightly bloodshot, tie undone at the neck. He has not slept. He is clean-shaven, a mountain of nervous energy. He has a TV set and a radio, and he is following the news closely. He has seen Abdul Wakil's press conference that evening, in which Wakil accused him of being "a hated dictator," and tried to distance himself from Najib. Meanwhile, in the corridors I can hear General

Toukhi's children scurrying about. His oldest son, polite and handsome, around fourteen years old, brings us tea. Najib is glad to see me. He saw me on local TV, at a meeting with Wakil. The camera had focused on me, "a U.S. citizen and senior UN official recently arrived in Kabul." [In other words, the usual suspect, a spy who had been sent by his government to show its concern for the deteriorating situation.]

I tell Najib that Wakil was inflexible, and talked bitterly about the "illegality" of Najib's resignation. He asked why the Watan Party and the government had not been consulted prior to Najib's resignation and attempted escape.

Though Najib's English is broken, he can express himself well enough. He tells me that the night before his planned escape Wakil had come to him and wept at the prospect of Najib's imminent departure. Najib and Wakil had known each other since "sixth form," he says. They had served together in the Kabul government since the original coup that overthrew the King (in 1973). Under Najib's predecessor, Babrak Karmal, Wakil had been posted to Vietnam as an ambassador, a way of keeping him out of the corridors of power. In Vietnam, Wakil had barely been able to exist financially. When Najib had taken over, he had brought Wakil back, and installed him as foreign minister. Now Wakil had turned "180 degrees." Najib denounces Wakil as "a coward person." (Given Afghan machismo, such an insult is very strong.)

Najib asks why, if he personally has been such an obstacle to peace, there is no peace now that he has resigned.

At this point, Benon arrives. Najib is happy to see him. He knows Benon is his only hope for getting out of Kabul alive. Benon greets Najib and then sits down. Najib repeats to Benon most of what he has just said to me. Then Najib asks a favor. He has heard a rumor that his wife and children, now in New Delhi, had been asked to leave India, under threat of reprisal, and to relocate somewhere in Europe. Najib asks if the rumor is true. He has not talked to his wife since hearing the rumor. If it is true, could Benon arrange for security for his family when they leave New Delhi. "Don't worry. We can afford plane tickets," Najib says. Benon says he will inquire about the rumor first thing in the morning.

Then Najib asks another favor. He would be willing to have a public trial, with the entire Watan Party on one side of the table, and he alone on the other, to confront his accusers. Can Benon arrange that? [Obviously, like any good leader, Najib had collected information on everyone in the party. That was one reason they wanted to kill him.] Benon avoids answering. Instead, he asks about Najib's comfort. Has he eaten? Is he able to sleep? Does he feel all right?

---

19 April 1992

0710 hours. The days are indistinguishable. They run together like raindrops down a window pane. Keeping my journal is one of the few consistencies I have at this point. It helps me to build the illusion of order.

Today is Easter Sunday. The BBC continues to blare its blather. A few facts mixed with tabloid madness. Hysteria. One BBC correspondent, an ambitious twenty-five-year-old, recently told me that he receives a bonus each time his item is the lead item. He talks of an impending civil war inside Kabul. He is predicting another Beirut.

By contrast, Colonel Nowlan is reporting calm in Kabul.

BBC TV is showing pictures of rockets hitting Kabul.

But the pictures are two years old. Both the locals and UN people who have been here for two years confirm this analysis. They recognize the pictures. It is true there have been a few rockets in Kabul in recent days. But very few. And certainly less than there were in 1988, when the Russians pulled out. Or than at any other time since then.

So much for the integrity of the international press. The rotten media.

———

1000 hours. At the Iranian embassy. Meeting with "core" delegations.

There are rumors about someone being appointed acting president. Several names are mentioned. Voice of America is reporting that there is fighting in Jalalabad. Two cities north of Kabul are supposed to have fallen by agreement, without fighting, although it is not clear to which muj faction they have fallen.

The tables at which we sit this time are square, glass coffee tables, laden with pistachio nuts, cookies, dates. Tea and coffee are served immediately, brought in on silver trays, with pitchers of milk and sugar. No matter what the state of the world outside, there must be tea, there must be hospitality. And it is welcome. Certain traditions transcend even political disasters. I respect the Iranians for their propriety, their elegance.

[The threat of violence, of imminent catastrophe, is real, and one can feel it—in the tones of the speakers, in the guarded, tense movements of those present. In any case, one has to prepare for a worst-case scenario, and the history of Afghanistan is not one rich in compassion or magnanimity. Revenge, betrayal, and tribute to the conquering warrior are endemic to this country. They are, in a sense, biblical; perhaps more Old Testament than New Testament. After all, Yahweh punished and destroyed his enemies.

At the same time, Commander Massoud talks of peace, of coalitions. And Afghans are legendary traders. They make deals all the time. One wonders whether the warrior or the trader will win this time.]

_____

1120 hours. Still at the Iranian embassy. Delegations arrive. We move to a long, dark wooden rectangular table. Again there are silver dishes of pistachio nuts, pine nuts, English toffees, a block of dates, ashtrays, and polite waiters bringing tea and coffee.

Benon, as chair of the meeting, tells everyone that the UN is still pushing for an orderly transfer of power. He is frustrated; he is even prepared to go public if necessary, to push the UN's proposal for a Council of Impartials. [But he will not do that, I am sure; he will not go over the heads of the various factions directly to the people. It is only his frustration bubbling over. At times, it seems he has internalized this conflict, that he has absorbed it, and is wrestling with it as Jacob wrestled with his angel, except that in Afghanistan the only angel one wrestles with, constantly and inevitably, is death. For all Benon's repeated cynicism, he is deeply concerned about trying to prevent an all-out war. He is has fallen in love with Afghanistan, against all reason, and he is trying to protect her from being ravaged.]

Different areas of the city seem to be under the control of different militias at this point, Benon continues. The muj have entered Kabul. They walk openly through the city. They have relative freedom of movement. The Afghan government, such as it is, is doing nothing to restrict them. They have been here for days. In a sense, they have already "taken" the city. Kabul has fallen. But it has fallen to several groups, not just to one group. Perhaps there will be no need for the use of force in Kabul. Perhaps the trader will prevail over the warrior, after all. At the same time, there is the danger that the various factions will each carve out a niche in the city, a particular quarter, and use it as a base from which to assault other quarters. It is still possible there will be a holy war *inside* Kabul, which has already swelled to grandiose proportions from refugees and displaced persons.

[Kabul has so many neighborhoods, it is like a labyrinth. Like the labyrinth Daedulus built. For the Athenian Greeks all cities were labyrinths, and the area outside was jungle where the barbarians fought. Will it be the same for Kabul?]

David Lockwood, resident representative of UNDP, takes the floor. He has been in Kabul for about three years. He is a UK national, fiftyish, married to a Pakistani woman. Lockwood is fundamentally decent, reliable, and well informed. He says that as of today there are a total of 730 foreigners resident in Afghanistan, including some in Mazar-i-Sharif. He wonders what will become of them. And there is also concern about what will happen to the locals who work for the UN and the UN agencies throughout Afghanistan. Will they be taken prisoner? Allowed to go free? The UN must protect them, he feels.

––––––

1545 hours. At the Turkish mission. A spokesman for the ambassador tells us that eight envoys—from China, France, India, Iran, Italy, Pakistan, Russia, and Turkey—went early today to the Afghan foreign ministry to appeal for safe passage for Najibullah out of Afghanistan. Foreign Minister Wakil was unavailable, but the vice-minister for foreign affairs, Daoud Kawyan, received them. They were unsuccessful. Four of the members—China, France, Italy, and Turkey—went back again a few hours later.

Upon returning, the latter four envoys said that Wakil was still unavailable. Kawyan received them again. He had not looked good. He had been quite anxious, but had promised again to transmit the request to Wakil. A proposed military committee of four generals to take control of Kabul had not been formed, Kawyan said, but attempts continued. An acting president had not been appointed, as we had heard.

The main element in the government at this time is confusion. There is a lack of leadership. Meanwhile, daily life in the town continues. People go to their shops, to their offices. To the extent that there is an economy, it is virtually a barter economy. There is no cash. Currency values fluctuate so dramatically from day to day, hour to hour, that no one uses cash. Inflation is galloping ahead unhindered. At the same time, tea is still being served in the embassies, in the homes of the frightened populace, in the dusty back streets, in the refugee hovels. Everywhere there is hospitality, ritual. The mosques are open. People are praying. And people are starving.

20 April 1992

1030 hours. Briefing for several envoys in Benon's office. Responding to a query about the UN plan, Benon says the UN plan isn't set in stone. It never was. It doesn't fit into a mold. The main idea now is to avoid bloodshed. He says: "We are like the yeast in the bread-baking process. We try to bring all the ingredients together, and then when the process is finished, everybody enjoys the bread. It is up to the Afghans to solve their own problems. The UN is not trying to impose any solution." In fact, he continues, there never was a UN plan as such. It was an understanding, an attempt to set a process in motion.

———

1830 hours. Press conference at the Continental Hotel, Kabul. A packed house. Reception says sixty-two different news agencies have registered. Benon arrives a bit late and goes directly to the café, where he meets with three or four journalists, shakes hands, accepts to sit and have tea, and lets the press conference wait. He jokes, scattering obscenities like confetti.

At the press conference, he uses the "yeast" image again, saying the secretary-general got involved in Afghanistan not because he was looking for glory or to be remembered. The UN is only an ingredient in the peace process, as yeast is in the baking of bread. Nobody tastes the yeast, but everybody enjoys the bread.

As for the UN plan, it is not set in stone, he repeats. The secretary-general made a statement on 27 January of this year suggesting certain procedures, but that was not an inflexible plan, or a mold that everyone had to fit into. Besides, the situation has changed since then. The UN is trying to promote dialogue and reconciliation, and it has to take into account new developments, and adapt to those developments.

On 10 April, the secretary-general stated there was an agreement in principle for a broad-based Council of Impartials, but the UN has never insisted that was the only possible way. The Afghans themselves are the ones to decide. If the Afghan people want a government of only mujahidin, then well and good. That is their choice. This is a time to promote tolerance and forgiveness, not to take revenge. It is a time to achieve peace as expeditiously as possible. But the time is short; we may not have more than a few days.

The statistics with regard to Afghanistan are staggering, Benon says. Almost two million dead, another two million disabled; five to six million refugees. It is estimated there are ten million mines in the country. Afghanistan has one of the highest child mortality rates; three out of ten die before the age of five. In addition, the country has been totally destroyed. No one can possibly win this war. On behalf of the secretary-general, he appeals to all parties to stay in place, not to attempt any military advances, to give peace a chance. He welcomes the fact that an intra-Afghan dialogue is now going on. Any UN plan encourages that dialogue.

He continues: "I appeal to all my Afghan friends. We need breathing space. Please avoid anarchy. There is need for an orderly transfer of power. Almost all obstacles for peace have been removed. There should be a cessation of hostilities, a general amnesty, respect for human rights, protection of property, and the opening of all routes for the purpose of transporting food and other essential items."

Q: Where is Najibullah?

Benon: He is in Kabul.

Q: How do you plan to get him out?

Benon: This is a delicate issue and I cannot discuss it. But I will say that his departure is a part of the peace process. His presidency was a major obstacle, and now that obstacle has been removed. His announcement last month that he would resign accelerated the peace process. But please, let me ask, is anybody interested in talking about *peace*? It is the peace process that is important, not any single individual.

Q: Do you have plans to talk to other Afghan leaders, other than government officials? Commander Massoud, for instance?

Benon: Yes. I shall be traveling tomorrow within Afghanistan.

Q: What are the major obstacles to peace at this time?

Benon: Almost all the major obstacles have been removed. The last problem is to organize a new mechanism, one that must be decided upon by the Afghans themselves. No doubt there will be a transitional authority. The question is, who will comprise that authority? It is difficult after thirteen years of bitter war to agree on anything. The UN has no favorite individual or group. It does not oppose any group. The decision is up to the Afghan people. I am only a messenger trying to get different groups to agree.

Q: Has the question of participation in the new Council been decided?

Benon: I think there is a spirit of compromise now. There will have to be compromise.

Q: Was your role as a messenger hurt by trying to take Najibullah out of the country?

Benon: That was part of a procedure, but the procedure was not followed by certain groups. We did not plot anything. There was an agreement, and we fulfilled our part of it.

Q: Why hasn't the UN called for a cease-fire?

Benon: The UN never called for a cease-fire before now, because it would have been unrealistic.

Q: Is the plan for a Council of Impartials now outdated?

Benon: As I said, anything the Afghans want is okay. The UN has no emotional attachment to any idea. If the Afghans want a mujahidin government instead of a Council of Impartials, that is *their* choice, and it's okay with the UN.

Q: What choices are left at this point?

Benon: There are two choices now: either a broad-based Council of Impartials, or a council of mujahidin. The choice is up to the Afghans. Those choices are being discussed in Peshawar.

Q: Would a mujahidin council cause problems for Kabul residents?

Benon: The biggest problem is the composition of the Council. The idea of a Council has been accepted by all sides.

———

21 April 1992

0700 hours. Benon, Avni, and Colonel Nowlan are to fly to Mazar-i-Sharif in the north, to meet with General Dostom. From there, they are scheduled to go to Charikar, if there is time enough, to meet with General Massoud. Although Charikar is just a short hop by helicopter or fixed-wing aircraft from Kabul, one must fly over hostile territory to get there, and so Benon will fly the UN Salaam plane, a small craft, to Mazar, then fly two hours by helicopter to Charikar.

Benon leaves for the airport with envoys from Turkey, India, Pakistan, and Iran, a kind of "core" group, figuring that if he is flanked by government officials, he will be less likely to be harassed. In fact, they are all stopped, and then released. The entire group is held at the last checkpoint for about thirty minutes and searched before being allowed to pass. When they arrive at the airport, there are no planes. They are told that the air traffic controller, an Afghan national who works for the UN, had got "confused" and told the pilot that the plane was going to New Delhi. The pilot said he didn't have enough fuel for New Delhi, and couldn't fly until he got more petrol. In any case, Benon and his party return to the OSGAP compound within an hour.

[Whether the problem resulted from a genuine misunderstanding or from political machination was hard to determine. Often, particularly in developing countries, and particularly during conflict, procedures that were never completely efficient break down altogether. There are critical phone calls that can't get through, on networks that were never very usable anyway. One wonders if such phone calls—usually monitored—were ever made, or ever intended to be successfully transmitted. There are orders never followed because of factional allegiances. There is no such thing as a chain of command during a civil war in a developing country, particularly when ethnic allegiances run so deep. Generals in the field often have their own agendas, and since they are usually political appointees themselves, they must balance the political importance of orders given to them by a bureaucrat miles away from the front, against any military imperative or private goal. Moreover, during conflict, the situation on the ground may change suddenly. A hilltop changes hands, a bridge is blown away, a highway is captured, etc. There are procedures never enacted because new facts supersede the possibility of their implementation. In sum, the line between sabotage and ineptitude virtually disappears during conflict.

In this case, speculations are rife. Why did the pilot imagine the plane was going to New Delhi, the intended destination for Najibullah? Or was it the air traffic controller—who must answer to his national superiors, even though he is a UN employee—who "misunderstood" his instructions? Or was he given the wrong instructions? And who gave him those instructions? Or did the pilot and/or the air traffic controller fear reprisal if the plane were, in fact, going to New Delhi, and either of them were somehow involved in a plot to evacuate Najibullah? Was the air traffic controller acting on his own, trying to protect himself? And what about the pilot? Did it matter if those involved were Pashtun, Tajik, or Uzbek? And if the plane didn't have enough fuel to go to New Delhi, was that coincidental, or had those who controlled the airport made sure, as a precautionary measure, that no plane had enough fuel to go as far as New Delhi? And so on. Thoughts of conspiracy are ever present in Afghan politics. And there is usually some measure of truth to them.]

0900 hours. At his office in the OSGAP compound, Benon receives the foreign minister of Afghanistan, Abdul Wakil. [This is a highly irregular procedure under traditional diplomatic protocol. The foreign minister would normally receive a UN official. But these are highly irregular times, and Wakil is trying to save his life.] Wakil apologizes for the harassment at the checkpoint. Says it will not happen again.

0930 hours. Benon receives the interior minister. The interior minister is in charge of security. He also apologizes for the harassment and promises it will not happen again. Both government ministers say it was a "misunderstanding."

1100 hours. Meeting at the Iranian embassy with the representatives of several governments. We discuss evacuation procedures again. The mood is less tense than last time, but not completely relaxed. The Iranians are extremely polite and extremely suspicious.

1230 hours. Benon and his party depart for Mazar-i-Sharif, to see Dostom. They have no plans to visit Massoud in Charikar. There will be no time to see both, if Benon wants to return to Kabul by nightfall. He believes that his presence in Kabul may deter an assault on the city, or an assault on the OSGAP compound.

[One wonders if Massoud will be insulted that Benon visits Dostom and not him. One also wonders if Benon's presence in Kabul will be enough to forestall an assault on the city. But I can understand Benon's wish to be in Kabul. If the OSGAP premises are assaulted and Benon is not present, it will be difficult for him to explain his absence. Besides, if there are to be negotiations at the compound, Benon would have the best chance of negotiating with the muj.]

1700 hours. Benon and his party return from their visit to Dostom. They have brought with them some journalists who were stranded in Mazar. Benon immediately briefs the chargés of Pakistan, Turkey, India, and Iran. He is with them into the early night in his office. They come to him like the faithful, like messengers to the prophet. They must report to their capitals, and they must have the latest news.

The journalists who came with Benon from Mazar were Ed Gargan, the *New York Times* bureau chief in New Delhi, and three others, two men and a woman, whose names and affiliations I didn't get. The four of them had flown to Mazar a few days before, and their plane had been seized by local troops. They were left without money or lodging. I don't know how they survived, or where they slept, or exactly how long they had been stranded, but they had no immediate way of returning to Kabul.

[It is quite understandable that warriors will seize whatever they can, from whomever they can, during a war. And certainly a helicopter is a strategic asset, particularly in mountainous terrain where fixed-wing aircraft cannot always land. But it is not merely the need to survive, or to fight more efficiently, that motivates the seizure of strategic assets—food, shelter, and clothing included—during a war, particularly in developing countries. There is also a residual anger, a palpable resentment, among those who are certain of nothing—not even their homes, safety for their children, fuel for the winter, or cash to buy cooking oil, even when they grow their own vegetables and have their own chickens and pigs and goats—against the light-skinned angels from Western Europe and North America who are only passing through in the name of humanitarian idealism and will soon return to their relative luxury. The local people see as provocative the arrival of saviors from rich countries, brandishing high-tech communications gear and expensive vehicles and flashy clothes, saviors who enjoy the indigenous, traditional hospitality of the locals, eat their food, savor their culture, have sex, and then depart, leaving nothing behind but shell casings and waste and empty promises. They know that when the foreign troops depart to resume their bountiful lifestyles, they themselves will return to ignoble poverty. It is only the rich who think there can be nobility in poverty. In fact, for the poor, their standard of living will be even lower than it was before the war started, because what little infrastructure they had will have been largely destroyed, looted. Perhaps in future the international community will face up to this problem, and make some arrangement to leave behind a portion of the material goods that peacekeeping missions have brought in.]

———

The scene at Kabul airport for Benon's return is memorable. Two helicopter gunships precede the landing of the UN plane. One fires an anti-Stinger missile at a nearby mountain. We see the flash, then the smoke. The troops controlling the airport are under the command of General Mageed, who is the adjutant to General Dostom. It has been reported that these troops have formed an alliance with General Massoud. But alliances shift and change, come together and come apart. The best guarantee of Benon's safety is that he has just met with Dostom, and no doubt Dostom contacted Mageed and told him to allow Benon to land safely. But nothing is certain now in Kabul, or anywhere else in Afghanistan.

The airport troops are Jaujani, which means they come from Jaujan province in the north. Ethnically they are Uzbeks, reputedly the fiercest, most primitive fighting force in Afghanistan. Some are teenage boys. Some are, of course, older, and are veterans of a decade of warfare in this beautiful, ravaged country. It can be assumed that every single one of them, no matter what his age, has suffered losses within his family.

They are clad in various costumes. Some wear the traditional shalwar-kameez, a two-piece cotton costume with trousers that reach down to the ankle, except that in this case, the trousers have been rolled up to the knee, to allow them to run fast. Over the top part of the kameez, they wear long, quilted corduroy capes. On their feet they wear sneakers, sandals, loafers, boots. Some wear fatigue shirts. On their heads, they wear turbans or Pakul caps. And they all have gun belts and colorful sashes. Most of them have moustaches. They enjoy posing for pictures.

[Unfortunately, my camera was broken at this point. It was an accident I shall never forget. I usually carry inexpensive "idiot" cameras with me when I travel. If they are stolen, if they break, so what? Buy another one. But this time I was terribly disappointed. To see those soldiers, among the best in the world when it came to guerrilla warfare, so simply clad, so young, so shy yet fierce, was a sight to behold. Those who took photos of course asked permission first. We would never have taken photos without the permission of the general. In any case, the general agreed, and the troops posed.]

I receive a briefing from Colonel Nowlan and Avni about what went on in Mazar. Benon and his party had met with about sixty leaders, in various ethnic dress, and sat around several small card tables in the airport lounge. Benon was at the head table and spoke in English. An interpreter translated into Dari. No microphones. The leaders said that they supported the UN, but now that the UN plan had failed, they wanted to know what the UN would do next. Benon repeated his position that it was up to the Afghans. The UN was there to help the Afghans make their own decisions. It was their choice, their country. The UN wanted to help. Colonel Nowlan described the scene as "rent-a-crowd." Avni said the political organization seemed to be "Soviet"; i.e., along the lines that the Soviets had set up before they withdrew from Afghanistan two years before. [I wondered what Benon had expected to achieve with his last-minute appeal. Had he really expected Dostom to change his policy, his strategy, his ambition, after one visit from a UN official, when for months UN officials had avoided visiting Dostom or any other field commander?]

22 April 1992

1200 hours. Benon has left again for Mazar and Charikar. I spend two or three hours during the morning on patrol with the MILADS (military advisors). We drive through various neighborhoods in Kabul. We do not fear for our safety. People wave to us. They are friendly, always polite. Life goes on.

We see many men, young men, with weapons, walking through the streets.

I realize, when I return from lunch, that the government soldiers who are stationed outside the gates of the OSGAP premises have exchanged their uniforms for civilian clothes. Apparently they don't want to be identified with the government. I wonder if they will disappear completely by tomorrow.

1520 hours. I receive a call from David Lockwood, UNDP, telling me that the ICRC (Red Cross) has just reported to him that one of its field nurses has been fatally shot in the head by a lone gunman in the village of Maidan Shahr. The gunman has been arrested. He said that his mullah had told him to kill non-Muslims. Journalists are already on the scene. David suggests we activate our security net and notify core delegations, who can then notify others. I call the representatives of Pakistan, Russia, and Iran. David calls the representatives of India, China, and Italy.

One of our military advisers goes to ICRC headquarters, here in Kabul. He is told that the victim was male, an Irish citizen, who spoke Danish and seemed to have come here from Denmark, though details are not yet clear. He had been riding in the front seat of a vehicle when the assailant stopped the car, poked his gun inside the vehicle, and shot, without asking any questions.

I first call the representative of Pakistan, but get the name of the village wrong. I say it is Miram Shah. The Pakistan chargé, a man with years of experience in the region, a man regarded as the dean of diplomats in the area, says, "Why, that village is in Pakistan." I am terribly embarrassed. I call Lockwood back to get the correct name of the village. Then I call the Pakistan embassy again, and correct myself. The chargé is gracious about my error. [But he later reports it to Benon, who reproaches me.]

Next, I call the Iranian mission. The Iranian chargé is not at his desk, but I leave the message with his secretary, who assures me he will pass it on. A few minutes later I receive a call from the Iranian secretary: "I gave your message to the chargé, and he said that we had nothing to do with it." I laugh. Another case of realistic paranoia.

————

1630 hours. Lockwood calls to say his man in Mazar said the weather was so bad that Benon and his party could not fly back to Mazar (Dostom's headquarters) from Charikar (Massoud's headquarters), and therefore will have to spend the night in Charikar. Apparently, Benon flew the UN plane to Mazar, then flew by helicopter to Charikar, taking the UN pilot with him. "So now we have a plane in Mazar, but no pilot," Lockwood says.

[I think it is a good idea for Benon to be visiting the field commanders. If possible, he should even try to meet with Hekmatyar, who hates the UN in general, and Benon in particular. The various field commanders are politically influential; their military actions fuel the political process.

It is the same in every war. The military commanders in Afghanistan, not the political negotiators in Peshawar, are the ones who make things happen. But diplomats have a way of frequenting hotels and embassies rather than military camps, even though, until the very last stage, hotel diplomacy is always less effective than field diplomacy.]

Meanwhile, as it turns out, Lockwood's information from Mazar is wrong, and Benon returns safely to Kabul at around 1900 hours.

———

2100 hours. Meeting at the office of Foreign Minister Abdul Wakil. I accompany Benon.

Benon: I went yesterday to see Dostom in Mazar, and today to visit Massoud in Charikar. I told them: no more war. There are only two ways of entering Kabul: fighting or talking. The best way is to talk and go together as brothers. Massoud said he would not attack Kabul. There was no need to fight. But he said he could not allow others to penetrate the security zone of Kabul.

Wakil: The Afghan parliament refused the resignation of Najib. It was unconstitutional. Therefore, no one has to be appointed to replace him. There is no acting president.

Benon: Massoud wants to be represented in the central government. He believes that all ethnic groups should be proportionately represented.

Wakil: I am in touch with Hekmatyar. He is reasonable, but . . . I believe that we should all support the UN peace process. Hekmatyar does not trust the UN. The problem is that ISI (Pakistan's intelligence agency) is still provoking hostility. They are supporting Hekmatyar. Coalitions are forming everywhere in Afghanistan to find a peaceful solu-

tion, but ISI is trying to destroy the peace process. They
want conquest. Please, Benon, you must do something
about this. Everyone is for peace except Pakistan. There
are already *shura* (councils) in Jalalabad, Kandahar, and
other cities. There are coalitions forming, but Hekmatyar
and Pakistan are unwilling to recognize those coalitions.
Only yesterday we spoke to Hekmatyar's people. *They*
want to avoid violence, but ISI is undermining them.

Benon: I told Massoud that the UN only wanted peace. We
have accomplished our main objectives already. There was
a demand to get Najibullah to resign. Done. A demand for
a transfer of power. Done. A demand for establishing a
Council of Impartials. Agreed. We are ready for peace.

Wakil: The only one who opposes peace is Hekmatyar.

[Although Wakil's refrain about Hekmatyar's opposition
might seem simplistic, it was largely true, in that Hekmatyar (and
by extension, Pakistan) provided the major military opposition to
the assumption of power in Afghanistan by any broad coalition
that might not promote Pakistan's national interests first and
foremost. Hekmatyar was even opposed to certain muj groups.
He represented Pakistan (and Saudi Arabia), and Pakistan wanted
complete control, nothing less. Rubin notes: "The ISI had made a
tremendous investment in Hekmatyar over the years and
regarded him as the key guarantor of Pakistani interests in
Afghanistan."[9] On occasion, Rubin continues, Pakistan had even
tried to undermine U.S.-U.S.S.R. efforts, if those efforts conflicted
with Pakistan's national goals. "The ISI tried to use Hekmatyar's
militia several times in pursuit of a military victory that would pre-
empt the U.S.-Soviet negotiations and prevent the ISI's client
from being sidelined."[10]]

23 April 1992

1300 hours. Islamabad. I have come to Islamabad with Benon and Andrew. The SG is scheduled to arrive in Islamabad today. Benon will talk to him about the situation in Afghanistan.

There is no room for me at Canada House, where I stayed last time I was in Islamabad. So I have made my own arrangements, secured a room at Park View Inn, about eight kilometers from the office. Very few people on the streets speak English.

I have no local currency, no reliable means of transport. Had lunch at the OSGAP compound before going to my hotel, but didn't have enough money for dinner, and don't especially want to charge a meal at the hotel. Found a small market nearby. Was able to buy some diet Coke, almonds, and fruit. The merchant said he would trust me to pay when I obtained local currency. He cannot accept dollars. I was very touched by his trust. He had never seen me before.

Tomorrow I will begin to make arrangements for my trip back to New York. I am eager to see my daughter, Meghan, graduate from the University of Wisconsin. She made Phi Beta Kappa in her junior year. She is bright and beautiful, and will be a welcome sight.

25 April 1992

The newscasts are saying that Kabul has officially fallen today. Hundreds of mujahidin are in the city and have taken over government buildings, the radio station,

etc. Government troops have gone over to Massoud, but
Massoud has not entered the city. They have thrown away
their uniforms. General Azimi has told his soldiers to
pledge their allegiance to Massoud. There are reports of
scattered fighting among different muj factions, but they
are unconfirmed. Most of the shooting is reported to be the
firing of guns in the air, celebrating the fall of the communist government in Kabul. Young men are said to be running through the streets shouting *God is Great!*

Meanwhile, muj leaders in Peshawar have announced
agreement (the Peshawar Accords) on a fifty-one-man "transitional government" to take power for about two months,
until a Loya Jirga can be convened to appoint an interim
government and prepare for elections. (This group of fifty-
one is their alternative to a Council of Impartials.) At the
same time, it is questionable whether all muj commanders
will accept the new fifty-one-man "government," which is
scheduled to leave Peshawar for Kabul in a day or two.

[Commenting on the Peshawar Accords, Kakar remarks that
they were agreed on "in a meeting whose non-Afghan participants outnumbered their Afghan counterparts, although Afghan
self-rule was the subject for decision." He notes further that "by
24 April nearly twenty thousand armed mujahidin had entered
Kabul under the cover of darkness.[11]

It was not just Najib who was being held hostage. It was
Afghanistan as well, although this time the kidnapper was neither
Russia nor Great Britain, as in the Great Game. It was Pakistan.]

26 April 1992

Eight OSGAP staff remain in Kabul. Four are at the
German embassy, in a bunker underground. Four are still at
the compound—along with Najib.

28 April 1992

A thirty-car convoy carrying fifty-one members of the Islamic Mujahidin transitional government arrives in Kabul by road from Peshawar. It is reported on local television, and on the BBC. I watch it at the OSGAP office in Islamabad. The transitional government takes up residence in a large building not far from OSGAP headquarters. There is a ceremony. One of my colleagues, a Brit, remarks that the arrival of this group in Kabul is like the arrival of Hitler in Prague. The chief of Saudi Arabian intelligence is present at the ceremony.

[I try to imagine what it must feel like to be an Afghan living in Kabul at this point. But I cannot. And one of the reasons I cannot is that I must be more specific, and I do not know how to be more specific. One has to imagine what it must be like to be Tajik or Pashtun, or a woman or a man, or a *young* woman or man, or one who worked for the UN, or one who was a soldier, etc. At this time, in this place, identity is so crucial that life itself may depend upon what group you are part of. To imagine being an Afghan is a luxury that does not exist here and now for an Afghan in Kabul. There is no simple Afghan identity. Individuality itself has been taken hostage, captured, assassinated, obliterated. You are who your conqueror says you are, not who you think you are, and your life may depend upon it. You are part of a subgroup, a political species, an ethnic entity.

And perhaps that is one of the most terrifying of all realities when a regime falls, especially a fractured, ethnically antagonistic regime: the destruction of individuality. How can I ever appreciate that? How can I, who has the prospect of escape, who can return to a functioning democracy, ever understand the quiet terror of an Afghan citizen at this point? Perhaps that is why the simple, beleaguered Afghan looks to Allah the Merciful at such times.]

_____

29 April 1992

Benon has returned to Islamabad after two days in Teheran with SG Boutros-Ghali. He returned to Karachi last night but couldn't get a flight to Islamabad until this morning. I spent the last two days in Peshawar. One of those days I went to see the Khyber Pass.

Don't know at this point if I will return to Afghanistan. I have the choice of remaining in New York. Or of finding another mission. I don't think the fighting in Afghanistan, or in Kabul, is over. In fact, I fear it will get worse. Kabul may be destroyed. Hekmatyar is determined to conquer the city and exact revenge. The only UN presence of any use at this point will be that of relief agencies. Eventually, if peace prevails long enough to hold elections, the UN may be called in to supervise those elections. Otherwise, the UN presence will be perfunctory, only that of a listening post. Peace in Afghanistan is years away. Revenge is still the order of the day.

I look forward to seeing my children again.

_____

On 27 September 1996, Taliban soldiers entered the UN compound, captured, tortured, and killed Najibullah, then hanged him in Ariana Square, outside the Presidential palace. He had been sequestered with the UN for almost four and a half years.

3

The View

from UN

Headquarters

Actions within the region during, before, and after the period I have just described were not without parallel outside the region. Diplomatic initiatives in the metropolitan capitals and at UN headquarters continued for more than a decade, at times with great intensity, in hope of avoiding what finally happened: the plunder of an entire country, the massive flow of refugees outside the country and displaced persons within the country, the evasion and betrayal of numerous agreements, dishonest representations by parties to the conflict as to their ultimate goals, and, finally, the summary execution of the country's former head of state.

Out of the tens and tens of United Nations documents relating to the situation in Afghanistan during the 1990s, I have chosen to discuss seven that I felt were directly relevant for a deeper understanding of the incidents described in this book. I have attempted to analyze these documents in a way that penetrates their nomenclature and protocol, and elucidates the motivations and machinations of the various players. Obviously, I have not tried to provide a comprehensive survey of UN documentation relating to the conflict in Afghanistan, because that is not the subject of this book. Such commentary on UN documentation, and on the conflict itself, can be found elsewhere. At the same time, I hope that what is provided in this section, and throughout this book, cannot be found elsewhere.

I have considered the seven documents in chronological order, but I have not restricted myself to the time frame of my presence in the region. Quite simply, certain key documents issued prior to my arrival provide the basis for a broader understanding of the events in which I participated. They also help to comprehend how the UN system operates. With the best of intentions, I have attempted to explicate respectfully a small portion of what is too often dismissed disrespectfully as doublespeak.

Almost a year before I arrived in the region, on 21 May 1991, the then secretary-general, Javier Pérez de Cuéllar, issued a statement on his efforts to bring peace to Afghanistan. In his statement he remarked that he had just concluded an intensive round of consultations "with all segments of the Afghan people, including political leaders of opposition groups and resistance commanders, based in Peshawar, Teheran and inside Afghanistan, as well as with prominent Afghans currently residing outside the region. The Governments concerned have also been consulted" (SG/SM/4568-AFG/30, 21 May 1991).

The phrase "all segments of the Afghan people" must be taken at face value. It was not a new idea, but the fact that it was reiterated in this particular statement showed that it was one of the main points to which all sides could agree. It meant that communists had been consulted and, by implication, would have to be represented in any coalition government. They did not have to be the majority faction, but they had to be included. Had Pakistan, Saudi Arabia, and the United States and their clients agreed in practice that "all segments of the Afghan people" should participate in post-Najib Afghanistan, perhaps there would have been less bloodshed, both before and after the period described in this book. Or perhaps nothing would have changed; but I mention the issue here, because those who ignored the secretary-general's appeal undermined any serious possibility for a diplomatic solution to the conflict.

Mr. Pérez de Cuéllar then elaborated five points, which became the basis for all future efforts to bring peace to the region until Afghanistan descended into anarchy a year later, and was subsequently conquered and scourged by the Taliban. Here are the first two points:

1. The necessity of preserving the sovereignty, territorial integrity, political independence, and non-aligned and Islamic character of Afghanistan.
2. The recognition of the right of the Afghan people to determine their own form of Government and to choose their economic, political and social system, free from outside intervention, subversion, coercion or constraint of any kind whatsoever.

Since the next three points are more extensive, I will excerpt them rather than quote them in their entirety.

Point 3 spoke about the need for transitional arrangements "acceptable to the vast majority of the Afghan people...that would provide them with the necessary assurances to participate in free and fair elections, taking into account Afghan traditions, for the establishment of a broad-based government."

Point 4 spoke of the necessity of ending arms supplies "to all Afghan sides, by all."

Point 5 spoke of the need for " adequate financial and material resources to alleviate the hardship of the Afghan refugees and the creation of the necessary conditions for their voluntary repatriation, as well as for the economic and social reconstruction of Afghanistan."

It was quite easy to be skeptical about these five points. How, for example, could one talk of "free and fair elections" (point 3) in a country that had never had them (elections during the communist period were hardly "free and fair"), that had no infrastructure to arrange for them, and where there was widespread illiteracy and a nomadic population that could scarcely be counted? The infrastructure needed to hold elections is costly, takes trained officials, works best when those marking the ballot can read names (rather than simply identify a picture, a color, or a flag), when they have the means to transport themselves to a poll station, and when they and their residence can be identified and verified by election officials so that each voter does not vote more than once, or that someone else does not vote in his place. Counting ballots is also a complex operation that requires experienced people, as well as extensive security arrangements. It is as important as voting itself—as the United States elections in 2000 affirmed.

[For a brief time in 1991 I was a senior member of a UN identification commission that was dispatched to the Western Sahara to determine a way to identify those eligible to vote in a referendum that would determine the future of Western Sahara. A decade later such a referendum has still not taken place. Significantly, the problems in Western Sahara were political rather than technical, and were related to the rivalry between Algeria and Morocco. In Afghanistan, it is hard to believe that a similar rivalry between Pakistan, Iran, and Saudi Arabia would not cause serious problems in any referendum, even after peace had been restored.]

In any case, preparations for a credible election, especially in a country just emerging from feudalism, are onerous, protracted, and very often regarded by the domestic population as alien, even sacrilegious. The prospects for "free and fair" elections in Afghanistan in the early 1990s were about as likely as establishing democratic rule among contending schools of piranha fish. But the inclusion of such a phrase in the secretary-general's statement was essential, and understanding why it was essential helps to understand the UN's role in peace operations.

To begin with, there was no better common ground for agreement on a future government among the various players. Perhaps each major faction felt that by agreeing to future elections it was buying time, time during which it might win a military victory. If such concurrence seems disingenuous, that is only because it *is*; but it is still better than having no agreement at all. Besides, the promise of democratic elections some time in the future has the potential for generating international support—financial, technical, and military. The alternative is ostracism from the international community, perhaps even economic sanctions; and every emerging nation, particularly a poor, war-torn nation, needs international support. Moreover, the pledge to hold "free and fair" elections does not mean that it must happen in the near future. The pledge can be considered simply as the first step in a process, a process that may take a long time, but which remains a respected goal. While the complexities of implementing this process may be daunting, every long journey, as some philosopher has said, begins with a first step.

The phrase "taking into account Afghan traditions"

provides a carefully considered qualification to the concept of elections. Democratic elections are generally considered to be a Western activity, as alien to some cultural traditions as blue jeans and Hollywood movies. The prophet of Islam was never elected. Nor were Moses or Abraham or Jesus, to name only a few of the men who have had an abiding influence on human history. (And for those who would argue there is a distinction to be made between the spiritual and the temporal, let them not forget that the Old Testament prophets were also political leaders.) In any case, there are those in Western capitals who circle the world proclaiming the doctrine of "free and fair elections" as if they were crusaders armed with the single eternal truth, as if the only path to moral rectitude consisted of submission to the divine electoral process. People in developing countries often regard these free-market missionaries as little more than the mendacious messengers of materialism. Both sides have a point. You can't charge into a country and tell people that their values for the past millennium have been corrupt and immoral, and that if they want salvation they must have a computer and a Coke. On the other hand, villainous despots cannot hide forever behind national sovereignty and tradition, and continue with impunity to perpetuate their lucrative tyrannies. For the moment, however, I am only trying to explain the reason for the phrase "Afghan traditions," a phrase that might otherwise seem gratuitous. It carries with it great emotion, and thus, must be seriously considered if there is to be effective compromise.

As for the phrase "broad-based government," it refers not only to communist factions but also to Muslim sects that have a cultural affinity with Iran, Pakistan, Uzbekistan, or Tajikistan. None of those, the secretary-general is saying, should be excluded from a future government.

One more comment begs to be added. Official political

statements, especially those that have been agreed to by the major players in an international conflict, must be taken seriously. In fact, they must be taken as being truthful. No matter how skeptical, cynical, or incredulous the observer or the interlocutor may be, official statements must be taken seriously or there is no basis for negotiation. If Najibullah says in an official announcement that he will resign, then he has to be taken at this word, and procedures must be put in place to provide for succession to his regime. Similarly, if the government of Pakistan says in an official statement that it will not intervene in Afghanistan's internal affairs, then the doubters may insist on methods for monitoring and verifying that statement, but they can never simply dismiss it as being untrue. Otherwise, there is no basis for negotiation. None of us on the ground in the region believed for one moment that other nations would stay out of Afghanistan's internal affairs, but we had to proceed as if what they said were true, and then try to build on their promises. To reject completely the assertions of individual governments would have led us nowhere. Better to shore up a weak foundation, or replace it with a stronger one, than to have no foundation at all. (No doubt there is an Afghan proverb that makes the same argument far more poetically.) Thus, the secretary-general's five points, accepted by all the players, were basic to the UN's presence in the region and guided our efforts all the while I was there.

———

The next document I wish to consider is the text of two statements, made on 13 September 1991. The texts were subsequently forwarded to the UN secretary-general on 24 October, and issued as UN documents (A/46/595-S/23163). The first is a joint statement on Afghanistan, made following talks between U.S. Secretary of State James A. Baker III and U.S.S.R. Foreign Minister Boris D. Pankin. The second is a commentary on that statement, made by the same two officials.

Significantly, these statements on Afghanistan came at a time when another event, which was a kind of pedal point to every major theme on the international agenda and presented the United Nations with its greatest challenge since the days of the war in the former Belgian Congo, underscored the need for U.S.–U.S.S.R. cooperation: the war in Yugoslavia. At the time, most of the fighting in Yugoslavia was confined to Croatia. The war in Bosnia was still months away, although everyone with knowledge of the Balkans knew that war in Bosnia was waiting in the wings like a vulture preparing to swoop down on the corpse of peace. There was hope in the international community that if the two major powers could reach agreement on how to resolve the civil war in Afghanistan, then perhaps they could reach an accord on how to pacify Yugoslavia. Of course, the situations in Afghanistan and Yugoslavia were different. The war in Afghanistan had begun before the Cold War ended, and had actually accelerated the collapse of the Soviet Union. Both actions were now post–Cold War conflicts fueled by nationalism, and nationalism was considered the new threat to world peace, particularly in former communist countries where it was being used to fill the vacuum left by the collapse of unscientific socialism. The hope was that if the explosive nationalist forces within nations, forces that had been suppressed during the Cold War, could be pacified after the Cold War, then it might be possible to make a peaceful transition to the new international order. Afghanistan was in some ways a test case.

(As for Yugoslavia, Baker was maintaining at the time that the United States was happy with keeping Yugoslavia together. A united Yugoslavia was a good idea, he was quoted as saying. It was a position that did not endear him to either Croatian or Bosnian secessionists, but it reaffirmed the U.S. desire not to become embroiled in European wars. It was an attitude that played well to isolationist sentiment in the United States, and even to a mistrustful Soviet Union, which was understandably wary of NATO expansionism. At the same time, it delivered a foreign policy issue to presidential candidate Bill Clinton, who picked it up and ran with it. With his characteristic opportunism and disingenuous enthusiasm, Clinton quickly became a passionate supporter of Bosnian secessionism.

As far as Afghanistan was concerned, Baker did not want the United States to become involved in a war in central Asia, especially now that the Soviet Union had pulled back. The U.S. goals in Afghanistan, as I was told by the U.S. ambassador to Pakistan, Nicholas Platt, were to prevent dope trafficking and restore regional stability. Nothing more, except providing humanitarian aid and helping the refugees return to their homes. In fact, what the United States worried about as much as anything else at the time (of course, Platt didn't say this) was how to control Pakistan, its main ally in the region. Military and financial aid to Afghan mujahidin had to be filtered through Pakistan, and much of it never reached its intended destination. It was appropriated, diverted, stolen, by the Pakistani military. In general, United States policy on Afghanistan was to have the UN take the responsibility for finding a solution to the chaos in that country, and to take the blame if a solution could not be found. The Soviet Union, meanwhile, wanted to complete its disengagement from Afghanistan and improve relations with the United States.)

Understandably, any agreement between the United States and the Soviet Union about how to resolve the war in Afghanistan had to begin by stating the issues on which they were in accord. Once those were established, they could move on to the more controversial points. Thus, the joint statement of 13 September begins by affirming the commitment of both nations to the Geneva Accords on Afghanistan, and by recognizing "the fundamental right of the Afghan people to determine their own destiny free from outside interference."

Both nations knew that the Geneva Accords had not allowed the UN to speak to nongovernmental entities, namely, the mujahidin, and that now the UN had to speak to the mujahidin. But the reaffirmation emphasized the key point that the nations that signed the Accords (including Pakistan) were responsible for honoring their commitments.

The obligatory statement rejecting "outside interference" was so vague that it could always be approved, yet never be implemented. One has to wonder, for example, what constitutes "interference." Military intervention is clearly a case of outside interference. But what about cross-border capital flows? Or military advisors? Or political advisors? Or information via the Internet, transistor radios, and underground newspapers? Even the smuggling of food or cigarettes can be deemed outside interference. What is the significance, then, of such a phrase? One important significance is that the phrase emphasizes the responsibilities of all other states toward the state in conflict and sets the stage for punitive actions against those violating the principle. What exactly constitutes outside interference, and what should be done to prevent it, end it, and punish it are matters to be determined during negotiations, but the standard must exist or there can be no coordinated international action.

The joint statement then calls for convening a "credible and impartial transition mechanism whose functions would include directing and managing a credible electoral process." The details and powers of the transition mechanism "would be decided through an intra-Afghan dialogue." (Repetition of the word "credible" suggests how incredible the proposal is.)

Imagine: "a credible electoral process" in a feudal nation at war with itself, on a mountainous terrain that reinforces tribal rivalries and physical separation, among an illiterate, warrior population. As said earlier, the difficulties, both cultural and practical, for establishing such a process were so large that the thought itself was almost surreal.

And yet, what was the alternative? The acknowledgment that such a process must be decided through an "intra-Afghan dialogue" officially protects the process from external meddling at the same time that it justifies international involvement. It is a call to what some sage once called "constructive engagement" among the parties concerned. Without such a call for self-rule via elections, concern by the world community would appear to be an intrusion on the sovereign right of a people to choose its own destiny. In other words, as fantastic as it might seem, the only ultimate goal that all sides could agree to work for was the idea, to quote the text, of "a new broad-based government through an electoral process that respects Afghan political and Islamic traditions."

The statement goes on to call for a cessation of hosti–lities and pledges that the two powers will "agree to discontinue their weapons deliveries to all Afghan sides." Moreover, the text continues, "They also agree that a cease-fire and a cut-off of weapons deliveries from all other sources should follow this step. They agree further to work towards withdrawal of major weapons systems from Afghanistan."

Once again, one may be skeptical about the practicality, or the sincerity, of such vows. But the text is significant for a number of reasons. For a long period, the Soviet Union and the United States had been unable to agree on what was known in diplomatic circles as "negative symmetry," that is, a moratorium on arms shipments to Afghanistan by both powers. This text is evidence that such an agreement has been reached. It is a major development. Furthermore, the statement affirms that "all other sources should follow this step." Although the usual suspects cannot be publicly identified, it is significant that the appeal is made public. Whether the other sources observe this appeal is a different question, but the appeal itself has political importance. Finally, the agreement to withdraw "major weapons systems" (read tanks, artillery, and Stinger missiles) from Afghanistan imposes an obligation on the signers of the text, an obligation that, if violated, could become a source of political embarrassment.

The commentary attached to the joint statement is important for the fact that it emphasizes the agreement on negative symmetry.

> Settlement of the issue of "negative symmetry," that is discontinuation of Soviet and United States arms supplies to the conflicting Afghan sides, is one of the crucial elements of this agreement. The U.S.S.R. and the United States agreed to cut off such supplies beginning 1 January 1992. They further agreed that neither the U.S.S.R. nor the United States will intensify arms supplies to any Afghan side in the interim.

The significance of the agreement on negative symmetry is that it sends a message to the international community that such agreements are possible. And if an accord can be made on Afghanistan, then perhaps it can be adhered to in Yugoslavia and elsewhere.

———

As noted earlier, the Soviet Union prevented debate on Afghanistan in the Security Council. Open discussion on the war in Afghanistan, therefore, was largely confined to the annual debate in the General Assembly.

The last debate in the General Assembly before I arrived in Afghanistan was in the fall of 1991, and it is particularly instructive to examine statements made during that debate by some of the key players, since the issues raised then were still the main issues when I arrived in the region several months later.

It is also worth noting that the General Assembly debate in the fall of 1991 took place about two and a half years after the Soviet Union had completed its withdrawal from Afghanistan (15 February 1989). Those pundits who had predicted Najib's regime would collapse as soon as Moscow withdrew its troops had been wrong. There was broader support for Najib than many of his detractors had imagined. Many still viewed him as a heroic nationalist standing against incursions by the foreigners (that is, Iran, Pakistan, Saudi Arabia).

The speaker representing Afghanistan in the General Assembly on 27 September 1991 was Fazl-Ul-Haq-Khaliqyar, that country's prime minister. Early in his speech he remarked, "In defiance of Afghan and world public opinion, unfortunately, some circles still harbor unrealistic hopes of achieving military supremacy, hopes which impede the commencement of intra-Afghan dialogue that could serve as a key for solving other problems" (A/46/PV.7).

"Some circles," that wonderfully vague phrase, most likely refers to Iran and Pakistan and their supporters. As a nationalist, the prime minister is appealing to national, rather than religious, political, or ethnic loyalties. More important is the fact that he decries the option of military supremacy, even though he represents a nation that prides itself on being among the greatest warriors the world has ever known. Afghan soldiers defeated the great British army at least twice during the nineteenth century, and only recently, during the 1980s (with the help of U.S. military ordnance), vanquished the forces of one of the world's two superpowers. Anyone who knows the Afghan people knows they have a well-deserved reputation for being fearless, tenacious, and courageous. Why, then, speak of preferring an "intra-Afghan dialogue" to the folly of "military supremacy"?

There are at least two reasons. First, it is politically correct to appeal for peace when speaking at the world's premier peacemaking organization. The prime minister would get precious little mileage out of calling for military victory. The more important reason is that the government he represents is losing on the battlefield. Winners seldom appeal to the United Nations.

The next point the prime minister made concerned which parties should participate in negotiations to form the next Afghan government.

> How can one claim to be a proponent of peaceful, political settlement and, at the same time, refrain from holding negotiations with the main parties?...If we ignore the Afghans abroad in the peace process, we shall commit a mistake as grave as those who wish to negate the role of Afghans inside the country. The defeat of repeated military efforts is indicative of certain hard and objective realities which should be recognized and properly understood.

"Main parties" includes Najib's (and the prime minister's) party, which is a communist party. How, he asks, can
those who support the mujahidin expect to have a coalition
government without allowing communists to participate?
"Afghans abroad" refers both to those millions of refugees
living in camps in Iran and Pakistan, as well as to those in
more comfortable exile in Europe and the United States.
This appeal is once again a nationalist appeal. While the
exiles in Europe and America and the penniless refugees in
camps in Iran and Pakistan may not be followers of Najib,
or of communism, they most certainly resent the ambitions of Pakistan and Iran. Moreover, Afghans in exile in
Western Europe and the United States must be courted as
potential investors in post-war Afghanistan. The "defeat of
repeated military efforts" are the defeats *so far* of efforts by
various mujahidin groups to overthrow Najibullah. These
efforts have been repulsed, but the prime minister knows
full well that they are gaining strength.

Later in his intervention the prime minister cites a
statement made recently "in continuation of several proposals offered by Kabul on a political settlement." His attri-
bution of the statement to Kabul rather than to President
Najibullah, or even to the Afghan government, is an appeal
for national unity (who rules Kabul rules Afghanistan),
rather than an attempt to assert the dubious authority of
the regime he represents. His government's sense of
urgency is conveyed in the first sentence of the statement:
"We are in favour of direct, face-to-face and unconditional
talks with opponents of the State of the Republic of
Afghanistan, because setting prior conditions would result
in delaying the talks." Such a liberal outreach would never
have been made while Najib's government was in control,
and had the support of the Soviet Union. But government
forces are now in retreat, and the prime minister is trying to

rally international support for his démarche while he still can. The necks he wants to save include his own. The Kabul statement also proposes that talks take place "in the presence of neutral third parties," adding that Afghanistan welcomes "the mediation of the United Nations or of the countries interested in the Afghan problem." This call for third parties is hardly magnanimous. What the Kabul regime fears most is treachery. It knows very well it cannot trust its opponents to observe an agreement without the presence of an outside authority, preferably one with military superiority. Those in Kabul are fully cognizant of the warrior tradition of humiliating and destroying one's enemy.

The prime minister then notes that "the Afghan president" (Najib is not referred to by name) "in reaction to the United States-Soviet joint declaration last week" (calling for a cessation of hostilities and a moratorium on arms shipments to Afghanistan) had proposed "the enforcement of a cease-fire throughout Afghanistan and the commencement of talks between the state and the Council of the Internal Mujahideen Commander, leader of the parties and groups based in Peshawar and Tehran, the former king and his followers, and Afghan intellectuals living in Europe and America." This broad-based appeal, this willingness to be included, even subsumed, in a wider group, would of course never be made by a government fully in control of its territory. And the fact that the Afghan government does not control the majority of its territory is also the reason for the appeal to enforce a cease-fire throughout Afghanistan. Not just a cease-fire, but the enforcement of a cease-fire. The words have been chosen carefully, since "enforcement" would mean either the stationing of foreign troops on Afghan soil, aerial surveillance, or both, in order to monitor and prevent unauthorized military activity. The forces that would be called upon to monitor any cease-fire would presumably be United Nations forces, but the details of enforcement are judicially not mentioned. At a time when Afghanistan is besieged by foreign forces, the prime minister is not likely to call for the introduction of more foreign forces on Afghan soil, even if they are under a United Nations flag. Moreover, it is the Security Council, which does not even have Afghanistan on its agenda, for reasons discussed earlier, that normally authorizes peacekeeping forces. In short, the prime minister's proposal to the General Assembly is completely unrealistic, and as such, is yet another sign of his desperation. Finally, the refusal on several occasions during the prime minister's intervention to mention Najibullah by name presages Najib's formal resignation six months later. It is already evident, as it has been since the Soviet Union withdrew its forces, that Najib's participation in any new government would be an obstruction to peace. Efforts are already underway to convince Najib to resign.

The prime minister then refers to the "five main elements" contained in the secretary-general's statement of 21 May 1991. He gives it unqualified endorsement as the basis, following a transition period, for "security, stability, democracy and development" in Afghanistan. He notes that the secretary-general's statement "represents the international consensus and was supported by the Republic of Afghanistan and all interested countries." There is no need to elaborate these five points again here, except to recall that frequently when I was in the region, I would hear Afghan officials say to me something like: "We support the United Nations. We agree with the five points of the secretary-general." The secretary-general's statement, thus, became a rallying point, a shorthand for those on the losing side. In their view, or at least in their rhetoric, one was either for or against the United Nations, or for or against the UN secretary-general, rather than for or against Najib. It reminded me in a way of the times when Palestinians on the West Bank would during protests against Israel wave copies of UN security council resolutions condemning Israel. In response, Israel would denounce the United Nations. Similarly, certain mujahidin leaders like Hekmat-yar denounced the United Nations and refused to speak with us, saying we were only trying to protect commu-nism and Najibullah.

The prime minister's willingness to form coalitions with forces being supported by Afghanistan's neighbors and longtime enemies did not completely eliminate his need to chide those same potential partners. He did so, of course, in diplomatic doublespeak, but those who knew Afghanistan knew to whom he was referring when he said: "If we put aside the personal interests of a few in the Afghan plan, and curb the illegitimate influence and hidden intentions of certain circles in some countries, the remaining differences are not so substantial as not to admit of a solution."

Good old paranoia. It is as endemic to Central Asia as it is to the Middle East or Eastern Europe. (Or to corporate boardrooms, for that matter.) And it usually has a basis, often a history, in hard fact. "The illegitimate influence and hidden intentions of certain circles in some countries" comes right out of the Soviet phrase book, out of the approved propaganda manual for referring to the enemy. It is a wonderful circumlocution, thoroughly Orwellian in its sinister implication, its perverse abstraction, and its men-acing, accusatory tone. How can influence be illegitimate, one might ask. Influence is influence, wherever its source. Influence from an illegitimate authority is still influence. And what about "certain circles in some countries"? Another delicious circumlocution intended to absolve the people, while indicting their leaders. "Some countries" might be Iran, Pakistan, Saudi Arabia, the United States. Who knows? One can never be too circumspect. But even within those countries, it is not all the people, it is only those in certain circles, that is, those who profit from war—imperialists, racists, reactionaries, and so on. In communist regimes, which at times seem dedicated to the destruction of language, name-calling takes on new meanings, plumbs new depths.

Yet, lest his intervention might be interpreted to mean what it is supposed to mean, the prime minister adds, only two or three sentences later, the following pacifier: "We also hope that the recent visit of the secretary-general to Teheran and Riyadh and his discussions with the leaders of Iran, Pakistan, Saudi Arabia, and with the two Mujahidin leaders, namely, Hazrat Saheb Sebghatullah Mujaddidi and Jenab Pir Saheb Sayed Ahmad Gailani may bring an added impetus to the peace efforts and prepare the ground for negotiations on the launching of a transition process." Maybe the secretary-general can reeducate our villainous opponents, in other words, since the struggle in Afghanistan is between those who support the secretary-general and those who do not.

The prime minister closes his statement by affirming that his country favors good relations with Pakistan, that it has historic ties with Iran, that it considers China a "major neighboring country," that it attaches "special importance" to its relations with Saudi Arabia, and that it is sure of its "ever-growing, traditionally friendly relations and economic cooperation with the Soviet Union and the Republic of India, which have always assisted the Republic of Afghanistan in its efforts to achieve peace in the country."

One has to wonder at such rhetoric, even from a politician. Was the Soviet Union's ten-year war against Afghanistan an effort to achieve peace? Or has there suddenly been a sea change? The alliance of India and Afghanistan, meanwhile, is an interesting example of how politics can transcend faith. Pakistan is a Muslim nation like Afghanistan. Yet, for obvious reasons, Afghanistan favors India, mainly because both nations see Pakistan as an enemy. It was to India, in fact, that Najib was planning to escape the night he attempted to leave Kabul. His wife and children had preceded him there.

In sum, the prime minister's speech to the forty-sixth General Assembly was a complex mixture of desperation, pacification, and supplication. Now, years later when I reconsider it, I think of what a friend of mine used to say frequently when discussing politics: paranoia is reality. Yes, of course. Especially during a war. And especially in Afghanistan. I was to see that with my own American eyes.

——————

When the representative of Pakistan, Mr. Kanju, addressed the General Assembly three days later, on 30 September 1991 (A/46/PV.14), he did not spend that much time on the issue of Afghanistan. He had his own priorities. After all, interventions in the general debate are supposed to be about the entire range of problems facing the world community, seen from the perspective of the speaker, and for Pakistan the problem of Jammu and Kashmir was of primary importance and received most of his attention. On Afghanistan, he had this to say:

> The heroic struggle of the Afghan people succeeded in freeing their homeland from foreign occupation. It also contributed to the current resurgence of freedom and democracy in the world. But Afghanistan remains in the grip of a continuing armed conflict. Recent

developments in the region have, however, brightened
the prospects for a just political settlement. Efforts
must now be intensified so that peace can be restored
in Afghanistan and so that millions of Afghan refugees
can return to their homes in safety and honor. The
essential element of any settlement in Afghanistan
must necessarily remain the transfer of power from
the present dispensation in Kabul to a broad-based
government representing the will and aspirations of
the Afghan people.

The "heroic struggle" referred to is the war against the
Soviet Union. Likewise, "foreign occupation" refers only
to Soviet troops, not to Pakistani or Arab troops inside
Afghanistan supporting the mujahidin. The mention of
"freedom and democracy" is a concession to the United
States. Such buzzwords engender good feelings among
Washington bureaucrats and insure continued military aid.
"Recent developments" that have "brightened the prospects for a political settlement" are the advances of mujahidin forces, especially those beholden to Pakistan.
"Afghan refugees," meanwhile, are Pakistan's first priority.
Pakistan is not by any measure a wealthy country, and the
presence of three million refugees on its territory is a heavy
burden, no matter how much international assistance is
provided for them. The phrase "present dispensation in
Kabul" is one of the most detached and diplomatically con-
temptuous ways I have ever heard when used in referring to
a government. Mr. Kanju and his speechwriter deserve good
marks on that one. At the same time, the phrase belies any
affirmation on either side that Najib's representatives and
those of Pakistan are willing to cooperate in forming the
"broad-based government" Mr. Kanju invokes in the following sentence. For Pakistan, "broad-based" means a

coalition of mujahidin, preferably those answerable to Islamabad rather than Teheran. No communists (or other infidels) need apply.

Mr. Kanju continued:

> Pakistan...has embarked on a series of initiatives. We have held extensive consultations with the countries concerned, namely Iran, Saudi Arabia, the United States and the Soviet Union. We have also fully supported the efforts of the Secretary-General. Pakistan and Iran have also resolved to work together with the Afghan mujahidin in a trilateral framework to promote the peace process.

This is merely a statement of good intentions and as such is thoroughly disingenuous, as are the statements at this point of all parties to the conflict in Afghanistan. But what is interesting is the apparent contradiction between consulting the "countries concerned," namely Iran, Saudi Arabia, the United States and the Soviet Union, yet resolving to work only with Iran and the Afghan mujahidin when it comes to promoting the peace process, as if Pakistan had informed the others that they should sign on to the use of a trilateral framework to promote peace, but otherwise stay out of it. One is tempted to ask what the role of Saudi Arabia is in this context. The roles of Iran, the Soviet Union and the United States are understandable. But Saudi Arabia? It is neither a front-line state, nor a superpower with global interests. Yet clearly the banker for the mujahidin and Pakistan must be acknowledged. And clearly the "present dispensation in Kabul" must be ignored.

Finally, there is the obligatory support for the efforts of the secretary-general, elaborated in the succeeding paragraph when Mr. Kanju comes out in favor of a "package plan of understandings on all the elements of the proposal."

He highlights, in particular, the need for a "transition mechanism, which is at the heart of the secretary-general's proposal," the same transition mechanism that was at issue when I was dispatched to Kabul seven months later.

The representative of Pakistan then reiterated his concern for the refugee problem, a paramount concern for his government, and made an appeal for aid:

> Pakistan has been providing shelter and succor to over 3 million Afghan refugees for more than 12 years. They have chosen to face the privations and rigors of exile rather than expose themselves to the insecurity and uncertainties caused by the conflict in their homeland. The recent decline in international humanitarian assistance has not only exacerbated the hardships for the Afghan refugees, but has also put an unusually heavy strain on our already meager resources. We call upon the international community to continue to fulfill its humanitarian obligations until favorable conditions have been created for the voluntary return of the refugees to their homeland.

What concerns Pakistan at this point is what in international circles is called "donor fatigue." There was war in Croatia in the fall of 1991, and there were the perennial famines in Africa. Both situations were among others competing for international assistance. After twelve years of trying to feed three million refugees, Pakistan still needed help. I was with them on this one. When I arrived in the region in spring 1992, the refugees remained a serious concern. They are still a problem today.

———

On 18 March 1992, Najibullah made a formal statement as president of Afghanistan expressing his readiness to resign once an interim authority had been chosen to replace him (A/47/128-S/23737). This statement more than any other was what occasioned my assignment to Afghanistan. It was the most important single public statement that had been made concerning Afghanistan since the Geneva Accords had been signed in 1988. Since the statement is brief, I include it here in its entirety:

> I have just concluded an intensive round of consultations with Mr. Benon Sevan, the Personal Representative of the United Nations Secretary-General in Afghanistan and Pakistan, concerning the Secretary-General's efforts to promote a political settlement of the Afghan question. I have given Mr. Sevan the assurances of my Government's full support for the efforts of the Secretary-General, in particular the proposed Afghan gathering.
>
> Furthermore, I have again assured Mr. Sevan, on the basis of the proposal of His Excellency, Boutros-Ghali, the Secretary-General of the United Nations, and the commitment I have made to the people of Afghanistan, that I will not insist on my personal participation in the proposed Afghan gathering hosted by the Secretary-General as part of the United Nations peace process.
>
> I agree that once an understanding is reached through the United Nations process for the establishment of an interim government in Kabul, all powers and all executive authority will be transferred to the interim government as of the first day of the transition period. As stated by the Secretary-General, the interim government should have the appropriate powers and authority that should guarantee the unity, safety and security of the Afghan people, as well as the

territorial integrity of Afghanistan. The interim government should also guarantee full respect for human rights, and organize and conduct free and fair elections for the establishment of an elected government of Afghanistan.

I fully agree with the Secretary-General, as stated in his report to the General Assembly at its forty-sixth session, and once again reiterated through Mr. Benon Sevan, that appropriate international guarantees should be provided in order to enable the interim government to carry out its tasks effectively.

I therefore reiterate my readiness to place the interests of the Afghan people above all personal interests, and it is my fervent hope that all other sides concerned will do likewise.

Having spent some years myself as a speechwriter at the UN, I can recognize immediately in this statement several characteristics of an official document. To begin with, it was certainly not written by Najib, by the UN secretary-general, or by Benon Sevan. It was most probably drafted in Kabul by Benon's staff, and after being approved by Benon, sent to New York, adjusted at UN headquarters to take into account the mood of the Security Council and the international community, then sent back to Kabul, adjusted again, and finally presented to Najib. From the beginning, Najib had been allowed input, but not a veto. Once he agreed to resign, based on assurances from the UN that his life would be protected, Najib was obligated to accept certain conditions. Those conditions are evident in his text.

The very title of the statement is revealing. When the text was circulated in New York it was entitled "Statement dated 18 March 1992 by the President of Afghanistan." There was no reference in the title to the government of Afghanistan, since the present government of Afghanistan was not about to resign; it wanted to retain its dubious legitimacy, including its seat at the United Nations and its membership in all international organizations, for as long as possible. By contrast, in his intervention six months earlier at the forty-sixth General Assembly, the prime minister of Afghanistan had referred to, and read into the official record, "several proposals by Kabul on a political settlement." The use of "Kabul" in that statement rather than "government of Afghanistan" or any reference at all to the president of Afghanistan was significant for its calculated intention to offend the least number of combatants. Najibullah's resignation, on the other hand, was a personal document, as opposed to a government document. Of course, Najib's statement had direct implications for the future of his deteriorating government, but its main purpose was to assuage those critics who said there could be no peace in Afghanistan unless Najib himself departed. In addition, though not stated, Najib's pronouncement assumed that the UN would provide assurances for the safety of his person and family when the time came. Otherwise, the statement would not have been circulated as an official UN document and would not have mentioned the United Nations as many times as it did. It implied UN protection as well as political endorsement. Unfortunately, however, it was this very same endorsement that allowed Hekmatyar and other Najib-haters to accuse the UN of coddling and protecting Najib. In that sense, Najib's proposed resignation may have fueled the determination of his antagonists and increased their mistrust of the United Nations even more.

The first paragraph takes care in stating Benon Sevan's full title, not only for the sake of accuracy but also because it reemphasizes that Afghanistan's problem is partly the responsibility of Pakistan. The war in Afghanistan is acknowledged to be an international conflict. The invocation of the secretary-general is, as stated earlier, an attempt to recast the conflict as though it were one between those who support the secretary-general (and the international community) and those who oppose the secretary-general. Moreover, the five points made by the secretary-general have been accepted by all parties to the conflict, and therefore, form the common ground for all future action.

The choice of the phrase "political settlement" cannot be overemphasized. It takes the conflict away from the generals and puts it in the hands of the politicians. It is always a welcome phrase at the United Nations, which is a political organization committed to the peaceful resolution of conflicts, and the phrase is meant to say again to those who favor a military victory that they are working against the will of the international community.

The use of the phrase "my Government," avoided in the title, is Najib's way of saying to his detractors that they must include his government in negotiations on his country's future. After all, Najib is addressing an international community of government representatives, and his government is still a recognized member state of the United Nations. His use of the term is more to assert legitimacy than authority or power. Meanwhile, in the first paragraph of his statement, Najib has already referred three times to the secretary-general.

The second paragraph manages to refer twice more to the secretary-general and once to the United Nations. Some of this constant repetition is protocol, of course, and unavoidable. And some is to make the current debate seem to be a conflict between those who support, and those who do not support, the secretary-general. The proposed Afghan gathering, Najib says in his statement, is being "hosted by the Secretary-General as part of the United Nations peace process." And Najib pledges to cooperate with the wishes of the international community as expressed by, and manifested in, the person of the secretary-general. Thus, in a statement that is largely intended to remove himself personally from Afghan politics so that the peace process may go forward, Najib tries to depersonalize the process by saying he is only doing the will of the UN secretary-general, as any responsible official would do.

The phrase "I will not insist on my personal participation" is another example of calculated ambiguity. At the same time that it indicates Najib's pledge not to take part in the proposed Afghan gathering, it does not leave out the possibility of participation in that gathering by the Watan, a communist party, of which he is the leader. That is what he means when he says he will forgo personal participation. Representatives of his party, however, many of whom are still loyal to him and who have no other place to go, might well take part in the gathering. It fact, Najib has always supported the idea of forming a broad-based coalition, which would include communists, to succeed him. Moreover, the pledge that he "will not insist" does not mean he could not be convinced to join in the proceedings if he were encouraged to do so, at which point he would not be participating in his personal capacity, but as the member of a political party. In other words, at the same time that Najib is indicating his intention not to participate in any future Afghan government, he lets it be known that such a decision is not irreversible.

The following paragraph, which mentions the secretary-general and the United Nations once each, is essentially the meat of the statement in that it sets out terms for the proposed political settlement. These are the specific terms that were elaborated by the secretary-general in his "five-points" speech of 21 May 1991. The main reason I was dispatched to Kabul a month later, in fact, was to assist in the implementation of the concepts contained in this paragraph.

In the next paragraph, Najib once again invokes the name of the secretary-general, and calls for "appropriate international guarantees." This phrase is more than obligatory. Najib, drawing on his own experience, knows very well the murderous character of vengeance and retribution in his country. He wants it prevented, by international forces if possible, not necessarily because of his great humanitarian concern, but because he fears that a victory by fundamentalists would effectively destroy Afghanistan. In my few talks with Najib, I must admit, I was struck by his patriotism. Of course, he was protecting his own self-interest much of the time. But I sincerely believed he did not want to see Afghanistan fall to fundamentalist fanaticism. He spoke to me about Afghanistan with such passion and intensity that is was hard to believe his only interest was in maintaining personal power.

The final paragraph of Najib's statement is fairly conventional, though it is interesting for its emphasis on Najib's willingness to renounce "all personal interests." This constant reference to Najib's person was carefully scripted by UN officials. In this way, Najib's followers might be allowed to take part in a future government, even if Najib could not. Though such participation might never happen, its prospect was an encouragement to Najib's party, as well as to those of other socialist factions. It was a way of saying once again that the United Nations was not summarily excluding any group from deliberations on a future government. One might also say that Najib's personal withdrawal was intended as a compromise to those factions that were intractably anti-communist.

Finally, as I read this document closely I am reminded of a comment by Stendhal, the great French novelist and essayist, who himself had been a political official. Stendhal once said that he admired the style of political prose. Surely he cannot have been referring to its prolixity, its frequent recourse to passive voice, its convoluted syntax, its relentless reliance on abstraction. But what he may well have appreciated was its calculated ambiguity, its tendency to make each point by going around it, its use of euphemisms, its preference for allusion rather than direct statement, and finally, during his own era (1783–1842), its preference for intellectual propriety. I do not mean to suggest that any of these qualities is present in most contemporary government documentation. But the province of what one historian has called "constructive ambiguity" is the stuff of official documentation. It is also the province of the poet, albeit with more elegant language.

———

Diplomacy moves slowly, and in waves. Before there can be an agreement, there must be an agreement to have an agreement. And before there is an agreement to have an agreement, there must be an agreement on who is empowered to negotiate the agreement to have an agreement.

Such stages are always too slow for those in retreat on the battlefield, and marginal for those who are advancing. The ability to strike a balance between the two forces is the essence of diplomacy, and it is in that context that one should view the announcement by Secretary-General Boutros Boutros-Ghali on 10 April 1992, of the agreement to establish a pretransition council in Afghanistan (SG/SM/4728/Rev.1-AFG/43/Rev.1). The council would take charge until the convening of a Loya Jirga. The Loya

Jirga would then appoint an interim authority that would rule until elections could be held. That was the scenario. A bit slow perhaps, but it was one with which no party to the conflict could quarrel.

It is worth noting here that the secretary-general was uniquely qualified to issue this announcement. Whatever mistrust the United Nations might engender among some parties to the conflict, none of those parties could itself issue such a statement with any credibility. It is generally assumed that the secretary-general has obtained support from all interested parties before he makes his announcement. Thus, if one or more parties to the conflict refuses to honor an agreement, the fault is theirs, not his.

The situation has changed since the secretary-general first elaborated his five points almost a year earlier, on 21 May 1991. In that earlier statement he spoke of the need to establish "a broad-based Government." But events on the battlefield have made it clear the mujahidin are not interested in a broad-based government, and as Mao Zedong once said, political power comes out of the barrel of a gun. Thus, the SG has had to modify his statement, without seeming to have reversed himself completely. The language he uses, therefore, is calculated to recognize the new reality on the ground, at the same time that it remains faithful to the integrity of previous principles which all the parties still officially endorse.

He bridges this gap between the situation a year earlier and the situation now by referring to an interim statement he made on 27 January 1992: "On 27 January...I expressed my readiness to organize an Afghan gathering with the participation of as many segments of Afghan society as possible, in order to agree upon a transition period and mechanism, leading to the establishment of a government through free and fair elections."

This time the reference is not to "a broad-based government," because he is talking about organizing a Loya Jirga, which will eventually lead to a government. And it is to "as many segments of Afghan society as possible," because that is the nature and tradition of a grand council. This council can, if it wishes, exclude certain segments such as communists, and include others such as exiles like the former king (then in his seventies and living in Rome) or expatriate dissidents. The term "as many segments of Afghan society as possible" is at once more restrictive and more expansive, because it is only an interim step. It is a wonderful diplomatic abstraction. And it is not a retreat; rather, it is a modification based on battlefield realities. Also worth noting are the vagaries of "a transition period," which does not specify a particular time frame, and the term "mechanism," which does not specify what parties will comprise that mechanism. Meanwhile, the wave pattern has been reaffirmed. The "segments of Afghan society," once chosen, will form a "mechanism" that will decide on a time frame, which will in turn lead to "the establishment of a government through free and fair elections."

In his second paragraph the SG identifies these "segments," and with the insertion of the word "all" announces his success in having been able to contact "all" segments of the Afghan people. When he had referred to "as many...as possible," he had signified his intent to be fair. He had not been sure he would be able to reach "all" segments, but in fact, his extensive effort has been successful. Thus, he states that Benon Sevan has carried out "an intensive round of consultations with "all segments of the Afghan people." They included "political leaders, mujahideen commanders, religious leaders, tribal elders and prominent Afghan personalities based in Islamabad, Peshawar, Tehran and inside

Afghanistan, as well as Afghans currently residing outside the region. The Governments concerned have also been consulted." These are the elements that should form a Loya Jirga.

In his next paragraph the SG confirms that he has received "the support of the vast majority of the Afghans consulted" and the full support of the governments concerned. The term "vast majority" not only legitimizes the SG's efforts; it also allows for the isolation of those who are not included in the vast majority.

The next several paragraphs deserve to be set out here in their entirety.

On 19 March, President Najibullah publicly stated that he would not insist on his personal participation in the proposed Afghan gathering. He also agreed that once an understanding was reached through the United Nations process for the establishment of an interim government in Kabul, all powers and all executive authority would be transferred to the interim government as of the first day of the transition period.

President Najibullah's statement of 19 March is a major contribution to the peace process. At the same time, however, it has also emphasized the need to expedite the process for the establishment of an interim government in Kabul.

Most of the parties concerned recognize that the transfer of power from the current Government in Kabul to the interim government must take place in an orderly manner, if chaos and civil war are to be averted. Accordingly, an agreement in principle has been reached to establish, as soon as possible, a pre-transition council composed of impartial personalities to which all powers and all executive authority would be transferred. An Afghan gathering will be organized at the earliest for the purpose of working out the arrangements for the transition period, including the establishment of the interim government in Kabul. The two gatherings originally envisaged will be combined into one. Immediately after the formation of the interim government, the council will transfer all powers and executive authority to the interim government.

Intensive consultations are currently being carried out regarding the composition of the council and arrangements for the pre-transition period. I am confident that the membership of the council can soon be announced.

An understanding has also been reached that once the council assumes power in Kabul, there will be a cessation of hostilities, a declaration of general amnesty to all concerned, guarantees of safety and security for all Afghans, respect of human rights, protection of property, and opening of all major routes for commercial traffic, particularly for the shipment of food and other essential commodities.

Appropriate international guarantees should be provided in order to enable the council to carry out effectively its responsibilities. It is essential that all Governments concerned provide recognition and support to the council as the legitimate authority in Afghanistan during the pre-transition period until the establishment of the interim government.

These paragraphs contain the essence of the SG's announcement and are formulated with extreme care. In the top paragraph, the phrase "as soon as possible" reveals the critical urgency of the situation. It is not a phrase used indiscriminately. The "impartial personalities" who will comprise the pretransition council are at the heart of the matter. The list of names of those personalities, or persons, varies from day to day, and just as it seems Benon is close to reaching agreement on the list, one or more of the parties reneges, and the negotiations must begin again. The list has become the main diplomatic battleground; it is the Kabul of the negotiating table, the prize none of the combatants wants to relinquish.

The SG knows it is the mujahidin, backed by Pakistan, Saudi Arabia, and the United States, who are muddying the waters, who are preventing the list from being adopted. But as a good diplomat he cannot say so directly. Therefore, he avoids assigning responsibility and retreats into the passive voice, a kind of syntactical surrender. To wit: if chaos and civil war "are to be averted"; an agreement "has been reached"; powers "would be transferred"; gathering "will be organized"; gatherings "will be combined." The most conspicuous property of passive voice is that there is no subject. No one is responsible, in other words. For a diplomat, this is highly desirable; for a writer or anyone with respect for language, this is an outrage, an act of linguistic cowardice. To say an agreement "has been reached" does not say who reached the agreement. To say that two gatherings will be combined into one does not say who decided, or who concurred with, this arrangement. At the same time, one must be aware that the international community does not want a strong secretary-general, one who would dare to assume responsibility that the member states, particularly the Security Council, have not directly conferred upon him. They prefer him to remain less than dynamic. He had better not use active voice.

This same paragraph contains the explanation for why I was dispatched to Kabul: to assist in organizing an Afghan gathering "at the earliest for the purpose of working out the arrangements for the transition period, including the establishment of the interim government in Kabul." At this point, the intention is to hold the gathering in Vienna.

The next short paragraph consists of two sentences, the first in passive voice, the second with its dependent clause in passive voice. I must insist here that I am not trying to be a grammarian, or attempting to parse sentences. I am only trying to point out that in this most critical of documents, at a time when an international leader (the UN secretary-general) is appearing before the international community primarily to keep them informed and to assert his sense of responsibility, his syntax sends just the opposite message. His syntax keeps telling them, *I am not responsible for whatever happens.* Why could the speaker not say, for example, *My personal representative is currently undertaking intensive consultations...*instead of "are being carried out"? Is it because he doesn't want to be held accountable if the consultations fail? And why can't he say, *He will announce...*etc., thereby taking credit for the success of the negotiations, instead of "can soon be announced" Once again, is this because he doesn't want to be accused of failure? Perhaps.

But quite the opposite may also be true, namely, that the secretary-general does not want to take credit for success. The UN secretary-general, in fact, is one of the very few diplomats who is reluctant to take credit for successfully negotiating an agreement, since all agreements involve compromises, and no party to a negotiation, particularly a sovereign state, wants to admit it has made concessions to an international organization. Imagine the UN secretary-general, for example, announcing to the world that he was able to convince the United States to sign on to an agreement that it had originally opposed, in view of the needs of the international community. Jesse Helms and other UN-bashers would have a wonderful time with that one. Such concerns make it far more judicious for a secretary-general to use the passive voice and not to take responsibility for having convinced a state to relinquish to an international authority a part of its sovereign rights. If such reasoning sounds convoluted, that is only because it is needed to prevent a country's constituents, particularly its armed forces, from believing they have made the concessions they have made. It is called snatching victory from the jaws of surrender.

The next paragraph begins with the same passive construction. "An understanding has also been reached, etc." In this case, one wonders why it is so dangerous to announce which parties have reached the understanding. Is it because those very parties that have reached the understanding are poised to violate it? Most likely. But enough about grammar. What is thematically significant here is the list of items that the understanding includes: "a declaration of general amnesty to all concerned, guarantees of safety and security for all Afghans, respect of human rights." Among other things, this list enshrines the UN's obligation to protect Najibullah's life and person. There is no way that the declaration of a general amnesty cannot include the president of the country, who is a number of times addressed as such by the secretary-general. The guarantees of safety and security for "all Afghans" include Najib's supporters, his personal advisers, his Watan Party comrades, members of his government, and others deemed loyal to him. This is a valiant attempt by the secretary-general to avoid the bloodbath of revenge that we all anticipate. There is no talk here of "war criminals" or the need to set up an international tribunal.

In his next paragraph the SG asks for "appropriate international guarantees" and recognition of the pretransition council "as the legitimate authority." Without saying so, the SG is exploring the idea of UN monitors, armed or unarmed, to help secure the peace. But since he knows it will be extremely difficult to convince the Security Council to authorize a military force for Afghanistan, he does not state the idea directly. At the same time, he appeals to the international community to legitimize the pretransition council. The UN, after all, is an intergovernmental organization, and government recognition constitutes the major component of international legitimacy.

The SG closes his statement with reference to the five million Afghan refugees, expressing his hope they will be able to "return to their ancestral lands, voluntarily, in honor and dignity." To this day, the number of Afghan refugees remains the highest in the world, higher than those from Palestine, Cambodia, Rwanda, or anywhere else. This appeal by the SG is more than perfunctory. He also asks for food and medical aid.

This was the last major statement that the secretary-general would make before the dramatic event of the night of 15–16 April, the event of Najibullah's foiled escape.

———

On 17 April 1992, shortly after Najibullah had been prevented from leaving the country, the permanent representative of Afghanistan to the United Nations, Waheedullah (no surname), issued a statement. It was transmitted to the secretary-general on 20 April (A/47/165-S/23823). It is the last document I shall discuss.

In his statement, entitled "Statement of the Republic of Afghanistan," even though that Republic had virtually ceased to exist, Waheedullah expressed his support for the Security Council's call for restraint among all parties concerned, and for the efforts of the SG's special representative

(Benon Sevan) to achieve "a political solution to the Afghan crisis." The Security Council had issued its statement on 16 April, a day earlier.

The Afghan representative's call for a "political solution" at this point was both desperate and hopeless. He knew that. As a player in his country's recent history, and as a supporter of Najibullah, who had himself taken and maintained power by force, Waheed knew very well there was no longer any prospect for a peaceful political solution. But he had to go through the motions, not simply because it was proper protocol, but also because he was trying to maintain what shreds of legitimacy he had left (and, incidentally, to save his own skin). If he had not issued a statement, his silence would have been tantamount to political suicide. It would have been an admission that neither he nor his government had legitimacy any longer, and that he was willing to vacate his seat at the United Nations. Waheed was not about to do that. He was fully aware that there were instances of governments having been overthrown yet still having retained their seat at the United Nations, and although that prospect was unlikely in the present situation, he could not discount it. Or perhaps he might be included in a new government. He had to keep open his options, as poor as the odds might be. Otherwise, as he had in the past, Waheed tied the issue of a political solution to cooperation with the wishes of the Security Council and the international community. Continued fighting, he is saying, or by implication, *revenge* after the fighting has stopped, would be contrary to those wishes.

With the clear avoidance of personal responsibility, and speaking only as the representative of his country, Waheed goes on to say that the "the Republic of Afghanistan is of the conviction that under the present circumstances with the stepping aside of Najibullah, the ground has been paved more than ever before for the cessation of war and ensurance of peace in the country." Thus, he carefully connects the resignation of Najib to the prospect for peace in Afghanistan. It was not the mujahidin, he is saying, who brought down Najib. It was they who created the problem, but it was Najib's resignation that paved the way for peace.

Cloaking himself in the respectability of the Security Council, Waheed continues by saying that the Republic of Afghanistan "is of the view that the statement of the Security Council on a political settlement of the situation in Afghanistan has no alternative." This sentence, more than any other in the statement, borders on surrealism. Its assertions are almost delusional. Of course, in the long run all conflicts must have a political resolution if they are to endure. But at this point in Afghanistan the only choice that was *not* possible was a political solution. This sentence should have been omitted.

The next two paragraphs, quoted here, are notable in a way that may not seem immediately apparent to those unfamiliar with diplomatic doublespeak:

> The State of the Republic of Afghanistan declares that in full compliance with the provisions of international agreements and conventions regarding diplomatic rights and immunities, it will not spare any effort to ensure the security and safety of the United Nations employees and the personnel of diplomatic missions and their full freedom of movement.
>
> The State of the Republic of Afghanistan will not spare any effort in cooperating towards the realization of the statement of the United Nations Security Council and hereby requests the Jehadi formations and local commanders to also cooperate in this respect.

Waheed's moribund regime is in no way capable of ensuring the security and safety of UN employees, or the personnel of diplomatic missions, or their freedom of movement. But this sentence is put here precisely for that reason. It is Afghanistan's way of raising important issues and asking the international community to take responsibility for them since it knows Afghanistan cannot. Clearly, Waheed's regime cannot protect those Afghans who have been working for the United Nations and for certain diplomatic missions and who are regarded by most mujahidin as traitors. By appealing for freedom of movement, Waheed is asking for roads to be open so that people can escape if they wish (as Najib wished to do but could not). This sentence assumes importance precisely because Waheed's regime is powerless to implement it. Waheed's regime may, indeed, "not spare any effort," but its efforts would be those of a straw in a hurricane. And, in fact, the issues involved are particularly important to United Nations forces, which, as I can testify from personal experience, are always very concerned about the safety of their local employees in such situations.

The final paragraph, which requests "the Jehadi formations and local commanders" to cooperate in respecting the Security Council's statement, is a last attempt to place blame on the mujahidin for the chaos that is likely to ensue once Kabul falls. It is also one more desperate appeal to the advancing mujahidin for mercy, an appeal nobody believes they will respect.

4

Seven Years

After

An Interview
with Afghan
Expatriates

I have not returned to Afghanistan since I was evacuated from Kabul in April 1992, but I have remained in touch with the situation there in various ways. In fact, it is difficult to fall out of touch with Afghanistan once one has been there, even under the most extreme circumstances, and even for a brief time. It is difficult to forget Afghanistan once one has seen the majesty of its landscape and experienced the warmth and pride of its suffering people. No doubt such a pronouncement sounds sentimental. But it is difficult not to be sentimental about Afghanistan once one has been there.

One of the ways I've kept in touch with the situation in Afghanistan is through occasional contact with Afghan refugees in the New York area, where I live. Just before the beginning of the new millennium—in November 1999, to be exact—I had a long talk with two prominent Afghans who had been in their country, before, during and after my time there. They spent several hours with me reflecting on the events of April 1992, how they appeared at the time, and how they appeared now, in retrospect.

Unfortunately, I cannot give the names of my interlocutors. They still have family and relatives inside Afghanistan and fear for their safety. Such anxieties should not be hard to appreciate. At the same time, when I told my two friends that refusing to disclose their identities might strain the credibility of my interview, they assured me that I could disclose their names privately to any scholar or U.S. government official who wanted to verify their identities. They are very real people. Their memories are real. Their passions are real.

The first interlocutor was a high-ranking confidant of General Dostom for many years. He was with General Dostom when Dostom received word of Najibullah's planned departure from Kabul. He was with Dostom when Dostom dispatched his troops on 15 April 1992 to seize Kabul airport to prevent Najib's escape. He was also with Dostom in Mazar-i-Sharif for several years after the Taliban invaded Afghanistan. Before that, he lived in Kabul. Now he is permanently in the United States. I shall call him "A."

My second interlocutor is a businessman who lived in Kabul in the spring of 1992. He had been there for years before. He left Kabul some years ago. He returns occasionally to see relatives and conduct business. I shall call him "Z."

Though my first interlocutor ("A") did most of the talking, both men were in agreement on what was said. Rather than separate their comments, therefore, I have simply considered them together, as "A and Z," except on one or two occasions. And I have remained "PC."

PC: I am interested in hearing your memories about April 1992. How did you regard Najibullah then, and how do you regard him now?

A and Z: Afghanistan was much better under Najib, there is no doubt about it. Under Najib, we could live in Afghanistan. Under the Taliban, it is impossible. Under Najib's government, food was distributed to the people free of charge. They could receive free medical treatment. Now people are starving. They have no social services.

PC: But not all the people were safe under Najib's government. It was a severe regime. There was very limited political freedom. Dissent was not allowed. You know that.

A and Z: Yes, that is true. But on the whole, Afghanistan was much better off under Najib than it is under the Taliban. Najib stood against the fundamentalists. They were our main enemy.

PC: Were you aware of the UN presence in Afghanistan in the spring of 1992?

A and Z: Yes, we knew about the UN. But we think the UN should have stayed around until Afghanistan had elections. The UN left too soon.

PC: But the UN was never in Afghanistan with force. We had only a few people. We had no weapons, only a few military observers. Most of the UN people in Afghanistan were with humanitarian organizations.

A and Z: But the UN convinced Najib to resign. It had influence. It had a presence.

PC: The UN was only trying to arrange for an orderly transfer of power. It did not support any side in the war.

A and Z: It should never have convinced Najib to leave so soon. He should have stayed until elections.

PC: Elections were far off. Years away. First we had to have a transitional council to replace Najib. Then a Loya Jirga, and for several months an interim government while we prepared for elections. *Then* elections. But all that was only possible if the fighting stopped.

A and Z: The fault was ours too. The fault was Dostom's.

PC: What do you mean?

A and Z: Dostom used to be a friend of Najib's. They were very close. Then Dostom became too vain. When he was given control of the northern part of Afghanistan, he began to believe he was the most important man in the country, that the country could not survive without him.

PC: Do you mean he betrayed Najib?

A and Z: Yes, he turned against Najib. When he received information that Najib would try to escape, he immediately sent several planeloads of men to Kabul airport. I ["A" speaking] was with him when he received the call. That is how I know what happened at Kabul airport.

PC: We almost made it to the airport. We were stopped at the last checkpoint.

A: Yes, those were Dostom's men.

PC: I remember that the officer at the checkpoint made us wait while he called his superior.

A and Z: He was calling Dostom in Mazar-i-Sharif. I was there.

PC: And what did Dostom tell him?

A: He told him not to let Najib through, and to make him go back. We assumed he would go back to his home.

PC: And what would have happened if he went back to his home?

A and Z: Dostom would have had him killed.

PC: Then Najib was right. He feared he would be killed if he returned home.

A and Z: Yes, that's for sure.

PC: But why couldn't Dostom have allowed Najib to leave the country? He would have been out of the way then.

A and Z: Because Dostom suspected Najib would still have power if he left the country. So long as Najib was alive, he would have influence. Najib had supporters inside Afghanistan, and one day he might return to power. Without Najib, his supporters were no threat.

PC: Was there any other reason Dostom refused to let Najib leave the country?

A and Z: Yes. Dostom was afraid of the fundamentalists. He was afraid they would retaliate against him if he allowed Najib to escape. They wanted Najib. If they found out that Dostom was responsible for allowing Najib to escape, they would kill Dostom. That was what Dostom thought.

PC: Do you think Dostom was right about the fundamentalists? And about Najib's power?

A and Z: Definitely. You have seen what the fundamentalists have done to Afghanistan. They would still like to kill Dostom. And Massoud. [Massoud was, in fact, assassinated on 9 September 2001, only two days before the terrorist attacks on New York City and the Pentagon. His killers were believed to have been agents of the Taliban.] And others.

PC: You know that General Yaqoubi committed suicide. He had been Najib's minister for state security. We were told he committed suicide because of the failure of our mission to get Najib out of Kabul. He had personally guaranteed our mission, and when it failed, he felt he had failed, and he committed suicide.

A and Z: No, no, no. Yaqoubi did not commit suicide. He had a family, and it would have been a dishonor to them if he committed suicide. He was a religious man. We knew him. He would not have committed suicide. He was murdered.

PC: By whom?

A and Z: One of his subordinates, who was a rival, and was ambitious.

PC: Was it purely personal then? Or was it political? Did someone give the order to have him assassinated?

A and Z: It was ordered by Massoud.

PC: Massoud?

A and Z: Don't forget, Massoud is a fundamentalist also. He is not secular. He is not as bad as the Taliban, but he is also a fundamentalist. He hated Najib. So long as Najib was alive, he was dangerous to Massoud.

PC: Are the Taliban purely an Afghan force?

A and Z: They are Afghans, but they could not exist without the support of Pakistan and Arab mercenaries.

PC: How does Dostom feel now about the decision he made in April 1992? Do you have any idea how General Dostom feels now, wherever he is?

A and Z: We know someone who was with General Dostom in Turkey, months after Najib was executed by the Taliban. This person was with Dostom when Dostom saw a tape of the execution. General Dostom broke down and cried. He had been very good friends with Najib. He realized he had made a mistake. The Taliban has destroyed our country. Najib was much better. Dostom regrets what he did to Najib.

PC: Back to the UN. Do you think the UN was helpful in Afghanistan?

A and Z: Yes, but it left too soon. It should have stayed until elections.

PC: And what about Benon Sevan?

A and Z: He made a mistake by coming too late to Kabul. He should have come earlier. A day or two earlier. Even a few hours earlier. Then he could have rescued Najib. Why was he so late? We heard that he was supposed to have come earlier.

PC: He was negotiating in Peshawar. He was very close to agreement on a Council of Impartials that would have replaced Najib and taken over power. He was going to bring the Council with him in a UN plane, drop them off in Kabul, and pick Najib up with the same plane. At the last minute, a couple of the mujahidin groups refused to agree to the composition of the Council, and Benon had to stay longer than he wanted to.

A and Z: He came too late. That was all we knew. We didn't know the reason.

PC: And what did the people think? About the UN, and about Benon?

A and Z: They thought the same way. They knew immediately what had happened, and they blamed the UN for coming too late.

PC: Do you believe what I told you? That Benon was negotiating until the last minute?

A and Z: Yes, we believe you. But the people didn't know that.

PC: Thank you for being so honest.

A and Z: Can we ask *you* some questions?

PC: Yes, of course.

A and Z: Why didn't Najib leave earlier? A week earlier. A few days earlier. Why did he wait so long?

PC: At first, just after he announced he would resign, he didn't want to leave. He said he loved his country too much. More than once he said to me that he was willing to make "the ultimate sacrifice" if it meant Afghanistan could resist the fundamentalists. After a while, when it appeared his forces would be defeated, he became scared, and he wanted to leave. I think it was not only that he was frightened for his personal safety, but he wanted to be able to organize some resistance to the fundamentalists. I think, and this is only my personal view, that he wanted to set up a government in exile. And of course he wanted to be with his family again. They were in New Delhi.

A and Z: Why didn't Najib leave by himself during those last few days? With a government plane from the airport in Kabul?

PC: Hekmatyar and other hostile forces controlled the approaches to Kabul airport. Najib would have had to fly over their territory, and they could have shot him down. Any plane flying out of, or into, Kabul airport had to have clearance. And we never knew who controlled the airport. It was very dangerous. A government plane would have had a tough time flying out of Kabul those last few days.

A and Z: Then why couldn't he have flown by helicopter, or driven by car, to an airport somewhere else, and flown from there?

PC: Most of the area surrounding Kabul was controlled by hostile forces. Even an unmarked car could have been stopped. Najib wanted UN protection. He wanted to be in a UN convoy, or on a UN plane. He was suspicious and felt unprotected being on his own. A bodyguard was not enough. And he was right. And the UN believed the best way to get Najib out of the country was with a UN plane from Kabul.

A and Z: Thank you.

PC: Let me ask you one last question. Will you ever go back to Afghanistan?

A and Z: For business purposes perhaps. But to live? No, not until the Taliban is gone.

Epilogue

After the

Events of

11 September

2001

It is virtually obligatory—and rightly so—to refer to the events of 11 September 2001 when discussing Afghanistan or the larger issue of world peace at any time after that date. The world changed that very day, just as it changed in August 1914, with the onset of World War I, and just as it changed on 1 September 1939, when Hitler invaded Poland. We are still assessing how it changed.

For the record, on 12 September 2001, the UN Security Council referred to the events of the previous day as "horrifying terrorist attacks,"[1] which, of course, they were. In fact, W. H. Auden's oft quoted lines about Hitler's invasion of Poland seemed particularly appropriate in the aftermath of the suicide attacks on the World Trade Center in Manhattan, and on the Pentagon: "The unmentionable odor of death/Offends the September night," the poet wrote. More-over, there were compelling and abiding visual images of that day of murderous mayhem, images that millions of human beings around the world were able to view again and again on their television sets, images as addictive as they were catastrophic.

In a sense, the tectonic events of 11 September provided a natural epilogue for this book in that they ushered in a new historical era, the same historical era that was forecast in these pages when Islamic fundamentalist gangs seized power in one of the poorest and proudest countries in the world in April 1992. The destruction of the twin towers in Manhattan and the attack on the Pentagon by fanatics linked to Afghanistan brought to an end, with cataclysmic perversity, the era of the Cold War.

Few would have predicted that Afghanistan might become the stage where the final scenes of the Cold War were played out. But it was the war in that country which hastened the demise of the Soviet Union, and it was the actions of a terrorist network with training camps and a headquarters in that same country that caused the world to realign its priorities, its alliances, to rescript its most-wanted lists.

Just as the past helps to understand the present, the present also helps to understand the past. The United States had continued to fight the Cold War for a decade after it ended, thus leaving itself vulnerable to a new enemy. It had prepared for the next war by fighting the last. As Sun Tzu once said: "In peace prepare for war, in war prepare for peace." But one must know who the enemy is when preparing for the next, not the last war.

The Cold War did not end all at once with a single battle on a battlefield, because much of it was fought in the mind, in the collective consciousness, as well among the empires of those who gained power and wealth in fighting it. The Cold War ended in phases. Early on, it brought détente, a virtual end to the threat of nuclear destruction, shrinking defense budgets, and an improved climate of mutual confidence among former adversaries. But even after the Cold War had been declared officially dead, there were still Cold Warriors. You could take the Cold Warriors out of the war, but you couldn't take the war out of the Cold Warriors. Powerful European American diplomats—Madeleine Albright, Richard Holbrooke, and Zbigniew Brzezinski, to name a few—whether out of myopia or a spirit of revenge, continued to view Russia, with its arsenal of nuclear weapons, as the main threat to world peace. They pressed NATO, shorn of its defensive purpose, to push its way up to the borders of the former Soviet Union either by absorbing Eastern European states or by destroying the one state (former Yugoslavia) that refused to be absorbed.

This anachronistic policy of fighting a moribund foe carried with it an excessive reliance on satellite intelligence (identifying missiles) as opposed to human intelligence (identifying persons), talk of elaborate and expensive missile defense systems (which would have been useless against a well-planned conspiracy involving twenty men with plastic knives and box cutters), and politically correct behavior for tolerating, even rewarding, people and regimes who hated the United States and were intent on destroying democracy.

But finally, on 11 September 2001, in devastating bursts of ignominy and infamy, in a bang not a whimper, the Cold War expired with the shocking realization that the new and potent enemy of civilization was neither communism nor the welfare state. The enemy was terrorism. And the target for terrorism was the humanistic values of the

Enlightenment, secular humanism, what Western civilization grouped under the heading of "democracy." It was destruction, not deconstruction, that had to be understood. Suddenly, and against its own will, the tortured, tenacious Republic of Afghanistan became the midwife for the bloody birth of a new millennium, the locus for developing a new historical perspective, the classroom for a debate on post–Cold War ideology. The time had come to plant new roots at the roof of the world, ideological, humanistic roots that would extend from the Hindu Kush to Wall Street.

UN Security Council resolution 1386, unanimously adopted on 20 December 2001, touches all the main bases in its hope of restoring order to Afghanistan. It does so, as might be expected, in diplomatic language, but only a close examination of that language reveals the real problems involved in the parlous transition from war to peace in a country that is virtually the security linchpin of central Asia.

In its resolution, the Council calls on the new multinational peace force (International Security Assistance Force, or ISAF) to "provide assistance to help the Afghan Interim Authority in the establishment and training of new Afghan security and armed forces." Security forces are the police. After a war, a credible police force is as important as an army.

Diplomatic initiative should always parallel military action, but in the case of the war against the Taliban that began in October 2001 the Taliban collapsed so suddenly that political planners were outpaced. Power abhors a vacuum, just as nature does, and as the Taliban fled, law and order fled with them. Though Taliban rule was perverse, it provided order, albeit a brutal order. From the atrocities of punishing women for showing an ankle, to the inanities of prohibiting music, television, kites, and short beards, the mad mullahs imposed a "legal" system. Once the Taliban fled, their order, however despicable, fled with them.

During a war, police are either drafted into the army or are called upon to perform the paramilitary tasks needed to sustain a besieged society. They must smuggle petroleum, weapons, food, cigarettes, whatever is necessary. They must also enforce loyalty and limit, if not eliminate, internal opposition. To the poor citizen, there is little distinction between the uniformed police and the secret police under a tyrannical regime. They are both ruthless and corrupt. When the regime is overthrown, most of the police flee, leaving a vacuum. Frequently, the new authority installs its own police, but they may not be very professional. This dilemma is serious, because without a police presence there can be no order in a civil society. Foreign troops cannot fill that need. They can't even speak the local language. There is an urgent, even desperate, need for a credible, uniformed police presence in Afghanistan.

Warlords return to power to fill the vacuum when there are no police and no civil order. They quickly become the enforcers. That is what happened in Afghanistan following the rout of the mujahidin by the Taliban, and that is what happened, to a lesser degree, because of the presence of international troops, following the fall of the Taliban. Though a warlord's authority is less preferable than that of a democratically elected leadership, it is better than no authority at all. On a scale of one to ten, anarchy is absolute zero. Someone must pay the teachers, someone must collect the trash, someone must turn on the water and electricity, and someone must protect property. There must be a functioning civil administration, and it must be protected by uniformed police. What Wallace Stevens once called the "blesséd rage for order" is nowhere more evident than in the minds of the citizens of a civil society. And if warlords provide such security temporarily, it is better than none at all. International troops will not be able to train and dispatch a professional police authority to all corners of Afghanistan immediately. In the meantime, they will have to support, and perhaps temper, rather than condemn, local arrangements for law and order.

The maverick psychiatrist Sándor Ferenczi believed that when the authority of the father was overthrown, he would be superseded not by women but by a coalition of brothers. That is what happened in Afghanistan when Najibullah was overthrown by hordes of mujahidin, and that is what happened when the disparate mujahidin were in turn overthrown by a fraternal gang of mendacious mullahs at the head of a movement called the Taliban. In that sense, proposals to restore the monarchy are proposals to restore paternal authority. Even multiethnic, multiparty democracy (far in the distance) needs a single leader, whether prime minister, president, or king. The search for stability in Afghanistan, in other words, must restore a father figure. In political language, no matter how decentralized a future Afghanistan is, there must be a central authority from which to be decentralized.

Perhaps confidence building is the most important component needed for bringing together disparate elements, whether during war or peace. Unless there is trust, there cannot be cooperation. Indeed, there must be confidence building before there can be decommissioning. Stability must precede disarmament, not the reverse. The victors may be able to disarm the Taliban, but there is nobody to disarm the victors. Besides, in the absence of police, the armed forces must keep order. If that means deferring police authority to a benign warlord until national institutions are up and running, so be it. It would be unrealistic to expect a sparse international force to disarm tens of thousands of soldiers immediately following a cessation of hostilities. Practicality must win out over abstract principle.

Another danger in postwar Afghanistan will be the urge to divide or partition the country between north and south: Pashtun to the south and east, and Uzbek, Tajik, and Hazara to the north and west. That was the danger following the withdrawal of the Soviet Union in 1988. It will remain a danger for years. Even worse, there is the possibility of small statelets, within or outside of the north-south divide. In other words, each commander with his own fiefdom. Clusters of different ethnic groups. Clusters of different cultures. Internal borders. In reality, this ministate sovereignty would amount not merely to an ethnic division but to a rivalry over which faction controls the opium production, the gas pipelines, the precious stones, even the dams, bridges, and roads.

The UN Security Council expressed its opposition to the fracturing of Afghanistan by "reaffirming its strong commitment to the sovereignty, independence, territorial integrity and national unity of Afghanistan."

Regrettably, however, there are still voices that favor breaking up Afghanistan, those who believe Afghanistan is doomed to be a failed state forever, and as such will always lead to regional instability. These voices are usually foreign, whether of contiguous neighbors or of expatriate scholars an ocean away. In November 2001, for example, Eden Naby of Harvard's Center for Middle Eastern Studies told a meeting of experts in San Francisco that Afghanistan should be broken into "allied independent states." She added, "Getting rid of the idea or concept of Afghanistan is very difficult, just as getting over the idea of Yugoslavia was difficult. There is a sense that this kind of thing shouldn't be allowed to happen, because it can have a domino effect. But I think the idea of Afghanistan breaking up has already practically happened. There is no common language, nothing common to all these people. The expected amalgamation of ethnic groups into a nation never happened there."[2]

Yet it seems inconceivable to most international observers that such proposed statelets could ever be economically viable. Or that each would become a member of the United Nations, or of any regional group, or would pursue an independent foreign policy.

At the same time, most scholars of the region feel, as virtually every Afghan I have met personally feels, that Afghanistan should remain intact. Here, for example, is the view of Afghan-born historian, political scientist, and university professor Alam Payind: "[Afghanistan] is a multiethnic, multilinguistic and multiracial country. Even when...groups fight with each other, they don't want to secede. Outsiders may discuss this idea, but there is no wish for division among Afghans."[3]

Although no analogy is ever pure, Afghanistan is the Poland of Central Asia. Its neighbors constantly want a piece of it. And its citizens are fiercely nationalistic.

Another problem in postwar Afghanistan will be refugees, but that will be more an economic problem than a political one. In the Middle East, the question of Palestinian refugees is primarily political. Many Palestinian refugees want to return to areas that have been part of Israel for half a century, but cannot. Afghanistan refugees, on the other hand, will be allowed to return to their homeland. The problem is that their homes have been destroyed, as have their roads, their shops, their villages. But the Afghan government will not prevent them from returning. At the worst of times during the past decade, the number of

Afghan refugees was as high as five million, about 20 percent of the total population.

In discussions leading up to adoption of the Security Council's resolution, several of the players expressed concern for the relationship between United Nations forces and the U.S. Central Command in its continuing military operations against Al Qaeda. But a letter to the president of the Security Council from the United Kingdom, which agreed to lead the international force for an initial three-month period, clarified that relationship.[4] In his letter, Sir Jeremy Greenstock, the permanent representative of the United Kingdom, stated that the U.S. Central Command would have authority over UN peacekeepers, so that activities between the two operations did not conflict. No such clear understanding existed between NATO and UNPRO-FOR in former Yugoslavia.

At the same time, the UN was careful to state that its forces were there to assist, not to occupy. By "recognizing that the responsibility of providing security and law and order throughout the country resides with the Afghans themselves," the UN satisfied a need both of Afghanistan and of the international community. On the one hand, the Afghans bitterly resented foreign troops and were willing to accept them only as a transitional force to maintain order, not as a permanent presence. Moreover, it was understood that foreign forces, even though invited by the Afghans, should not be stronger than the Afghan army. That stipulation would satisfy the central authority in Kabul, as well as regional warlords who feared that the injection of foreign forces would threaten their authority. In time, that authority must be challenged, but such challenges can well be diplomatic and economic rather than military, and can be postponed until national elections, which are still years away.

As for the international community, it welcomed a role of limited duration and scope. Foreign governments did not want to have their troops in Afghanistan forever. They did not want to be indefinitely responsible for protecting the Afghans from their neighbors—or from themselves.

———

Perhaps the greatest dangers facing postwar Afghanistan are the ambitions of two of its neighbors: Pakistan and, to a lesser extent, Iran. This view is not a popular one to take, especially since General Pervez Musharraf, Pakistan's president, who himself seized power in a military coup, has greatly enhanced his international stature, as well as his economy, by supporting international efforts to dislodge the Taliban and to combat international terrorism.[5] At the same time, General Musharraf was careful not to denounce Islamic fundamentalism, since he could not risk offending a minor but vocal element in his constituency, or alienating his banker, Saudi Arabia. Nevertheless, right up until U.S. military involvement in Afghanistan, Pakistan was providing training bases for suicide terrorists, and was channeling many of its young people into anti-Semitic, anti-Hindu, anti-American, anti-Western madrasas (religious schools), where every day they were fed a curriculum of the worst racist and sexist filth. Vicious fundamentalist ideologues, tolerated and often encouraged by the government, targeted non-Muslim infidels and anything generally post-Renaissance or suspiciously Western in the most irrational and apocalyptic terms. That practice will not end easily or quickly.

As for Afghanistan, Pakistani officials had repeatedly tried to undermine any government there that they could not control. More than any other nation, Pakistan benefited from chaos and disorder in Afghanistan and from the fracture of the territorial integrity of that nation, since it had long wished to annex parts of Afghanistan. By working through the Pashtun tribe (as a result of colonial partition. there are easily as many Pashtun in Pakistan as in Afghanistan), Pakistan long promoted cross-border ethnic identity rather than national unity. It remains to be seen if Pakistan will put aside its desire to control the new Afghanistan.

Pakistan's subjugation of Afghanistan had not been a hot topic in the Western media before the tragic events of 11 September. But once the war against the Taliban began, the facts began to emerge. In a front-page article in the *New York Times*, Douglas Frantz had this to say: "For seven years, Pakistan's Islamic government had been the Taliban's main sponsor, alongside Mr. bin Laden. It provided military equipment, recruiting assistance, and training and tactical advice that enabled the band of village mullahs and their adherents to take control of Afghanistan and turn it into a haven for terrorists. The impact was considerable because, after fattening its coffers with American money, I.S.I. was able to tilt the battle in Afghanistan."[6]

The extent of Pakistani involvement in the Taliban dictatorship became more and more evident as the war against the Taliban continued. It was not only terrorists that were being routed from their hiding places; it was information as well. Following the fall of the northern city of Kunduz and the capture of Taliban fighters, Dexter Filkins of the *New York Times* reported that "here in the desert was a large group of foreign fighters the likes of which the Northern Alliance had talked about for so long. The guards described the prisoners as 'Arab, Chechen and Pakistani,' but in fact the group appeared to be almost entirely from Pakistan."[7]

Arab mercenaries were also numerous. Northern Alliance spokesmen estimated that of 16,000 Taliban soldiers defending the city of Kunduz at the end of November 2001, about 6,000 were from foreign countries. The Pentagon estimated about 3,000 were foreign mercenaries.[8] Whatever the correct figure (probably somewhere between the two estimates), the percentage is dramatic.

Equally dramatic was the attitude of Northern Alliance commanders, who declared their intention to separate the foreign prisoners from native Afghans. The latter would be allowed to return to their villages, but the former would have to face Afghan justice. Significantly, this attitude transcended tribal rivalries. It didn't matter to Northern Alliance commanders if native Afghan Taliban were Pashtun or Hazara or Uzbek or Tajik. What mattered was that they were Afghans.

The fanaticism of alien Arab mercenaries stood in stark contrast to the legendary courage of the native Afghan warrior defending his homeland. While Afghans were willing to fight forever against foreigners, they would make deals with, and surrender to, other Afghans. Even Najibullah, when he was finally captured by the Taliban, believed that he might receive mercy from his fellow Afghan Pashtuns. Of course he did not, because Afghans will often punish the leaders but release the foot soldiers. For Arab and Pakistani mercenaries in Afghanistan, however, there was not even hope for mercy. This utter hopelessness intensified their suicidal tendencies. At a hospital in Kandahar, for example, eighteen mercenaries, almost all Arabs, with grenades tied to their bodies demanded medical treatment—only from Muslim doctors—and warned that, if provoked, they were ready to detonate themselves and anyone nearby. In effect, they took an entire hospital hostage. Erik Eckholm, writing in the *New York Times*, reported that the attending nurse at the hospital, Noorahmad Shah, who was diligently treating the mercenaries, said: "All of us hate the Arabs and other foreigners who were destroying our country."[9] In the ensuing weeks, nine of the terrorists slipped away, two were captured, one blew himself up, and the last six were killed in a firefight.

During the Taliban dictatorship, Pakistani mercenaries occupied the best houses and apartments in Kabul, exploited local Afghans as servants, and pranced about with their weapons like conquerors. Meanwhile, Arab mercenaries hijacked the curriculum for the public education system. John Lee Anderson in an article in *The New Yorker* reported an interview with an Afghan professional he called Dr. Rostum (not his real name), who had this to say about Arab influence in local schools: "My son...is in the eighth grade, and out of eleven subjects he has eight that have to do with religion or the Arabic language."[10] Like parents all over the world, what Dr. Rostum wanted for his children was a proper education.

It is hard to overestimate the hatred that Afghans feel for foreign invaders, or the pride they feel in their own traditions. Consider how alien the Al Qaeda agenda was for them: their language was different than that of indigenous Afghans, their culture was different, and their goals were different. In the heart of the Afghan patriot, the alien Al Qaeda network was no more acceptable on Afghan soil than Soviet *feringhee* (an opprobrious Afghan term for "foreigners") were. As anyone who knows the Afghan people will tell you, Afghans are among the world's most gracious hosts—but only for guests they have invited, not for terrorists bearing bribes and Kalashnikovs.

Any post-Taliban regime must be aware not only of Pakistan's historic ambitions but also of Iran's. In fact, recent wars in Afghanistan have to some extent been proxy wars between Pakistan and Iran. But Iran has been in the minority position. In working through Afghanistan's Hazaras (about 19 percent of the population) and Tajiks (25 percent), both Shi'a Muslims, Iran has sought to maintain influence by presuming to protect the rights of Shi'a minorities from the Pashtun (Sunni) powers that controlled the central government. Iran's ambitions in Afghanistan have been no less perfidious than those of Pakistan, though they have been less successful. The international community, insofar as it remains concerned about stability in Afghanistan, cannot ignore the dangers of Iranian expansionism.

––––––––––

The Bonn Agreement of 5 December 2001 sets out the principles and the practical procedures necessary for building institutions that will ensure a stable and democratic future for Afghanistan. The language is diplomatic and at times purposely ambiguous, but by examining key paragraphs and phrases, one can identify the main problems Afghanistan will face in coming years.

The Declaration begins with the words "The participants in the UN Talks on Afghanistan," and then goes on to state what it is they agree to. Fair enough. But one of the problems Afghanistan will face in future will be to redress the imbalance of power created by "the participants." In the war against the Taliban, United States–led forces were so effective so quickly that the political process could not keep pace with military advances. Consequently, the Northern Alliance moved into Kabul with its police force as well as its troops before international forces could stabilize the capital and put a temporary authority in place. That gave the Northern Alliance great leverage during the Bonn talks. As a result, the largely Tajik Northern Alliance garnered seventeen ministries out of a total of thirty in the new interim government, including the powerful posts of interior, foreign affairs, and defense.

The Tajiks, as mentioned earlier, are about 25 percent of the Afghan population. By retaining more than 50 percent of the new ministries, including the three key ones mentioned above, they would appear to have a disproportionate amount of power.

At the inauguration of Prime Minister Hamid Karzai and his new government, the emphasis was on unity. Reuters reported that Karzai was dressed "in a green and purple striped Uzbek robe and...shared the stage with Tajik officials of the Northern Alliance, leaders of the ethnic Hazaras descended from Genghis Khan and Uzbek warlord Abdul Rashid Dostom."[11] Dostom, for his part, had originally said he would not attend the inauguration because the Uzbeks had been slighted in the new government. Three days after the inauguration he was appointed deputy minister of defense.

The Reuters account continues: "The national anthem played as curtains parted at the back of the stage to reveal a huge portrait of Ahmad Shah Massoud, who was the revered leader of the Northern Alliance that defeated the Taliban until he was assassinated in a suicide bombing two days before the September 11 attacks on the United States." Finally, in the midst of his acceptance speech, Karzai broke off to welcome the powerful governor of Herat, Ismail Khan. Khan, a non-Pashtun from western Afghanistan, who has long had strong support from Iran. But stability in a new Afghanistan will depend more on a fair distribution of power than on emotional declarations of ethnic unity, since the former is the base upon which the latter is built.

To its credit, the Bonn Declaration addresses this concern, when the parties to the Agreement recognize "the need to ensure broad representation in these interim arrangements of all segments of the Afghan population, including groups that have not been adequately represented at the UN Talks on Afghanistan."

On another sensitive matter, the participants to the Bonn conference express "their appreciation to the Afghan mujahidin who, over the years, have defended the independence, territorial integrity and national unity of the country and have played a major role in the struggle against terrorism and oppression, and whose sacrifice has now made them both heroes of jihad and champions of peace, stability and reconstruction of their beloved homeland, Afghanistan."

The tribute to the mujahidin is significant in that it strikes a common denominator that can apply to different groups of holy warriors. It can be taken to refer to those members, primarily of the Northern Alliance, who opposed the Taliban in recent years, and it can also refer to those native Afghan Taliban who previously fought against the Russians and were later recruited by the Taliban, perhaps innocently, to overcome the factional strife that divided the country after the Russians left. Thus, many of the Afghan Taliban had joined "in the struggle against terrorism and oppression" when they fought against the Russians. But Afghan fighters were quite different from the despised foreign mercenaries among the Taliban, who clearly did not defend the "territorial integrity and national unity of the country."

In another preambular paragraph, the Bonn participants note that the interim arrangements are only a first step "toward the establishment of a broad-based, gender-sensitive, multi-ethnic and fully representative government." The welcome concern for a "gender-sensitive" government is an immediate response to the misogynist Taliban reign, but is not inconsistent with Afghan tradition. At several times during the latter half of the twentieth century, women participated in Afghan government, albeit in lower-level positions. In any case, a government that does not permit its women to be educated stunts the growth of its children as well as of its economy. This is a key provision.

The question of a "broad-based authority" is one that few will contest. But what exactly does "broad-based" mean in practice? Throughout the 1990s, the United States, Pakistan, and Saudi Arabia opposed the participation of communists in any "broad-based" Afghan government and thereby undermined the possibility for a political settlement. No Afghan doubted that the communists had committed atrocities. But history is never black and white, unless it is made in Hollywood (or in Washington, as the two grow closer), or in silhouette (which is limited by being two-dimensional). Afghan communists had been in power for almost two decades before the fall of Najibullah, beginning with the government of Muhammad Daoud that brought down the constitutional monarchy of King Zahir Shah in 1973. During their years in power the communists had continued the many economic, social and cultural reforms begun by the King. In the words of one Afghan professional who survived the communist years:

> When we were younger, under Zahir Shah [during the 1960s] and later under Daoud there were cinemas and theaters in Kabul and Kandahar, Herat and Mazar-e-Sharif and Jalalabad, and for ladies there was no pressure to wear burkhas. In those days, maybe one to two per cent of the girls wore burkhas...And they were not like the burkhas of today, which have come from Iran or Pakistan; they were more like long veils...When Daoud came to power in Afghanistan, the education was great, it was the golden time for

education. And at the end of his time he brought us a TV station...There were lots of books, as well, even if these books came mostly from the Soviet block.[12]

These reforms continued through Najibullah's regime, as did the building of modern roads, dams, irrigation systems, telephone lines, and schools. Thus, not surprisingly, in 1992 some Afghans supported communist parties, and those parties deserved to be included in any "broad-based" Afghan government. In fact, those Afghans who hated local communists often hated them more for being sponsored by a foreign power (the Soviet Union) than for being politically repressive.

The new Afghan government, as the Bonn Declaration affirms, must be inclusive rather than exclusive. It may have to include even communists, since there are still some around. It will certainly have to include former Taliban. And the distinction when dealing with the Taliban should not be between "extreme" and "moderate," but between leaders and followers, between war criminals and those who went along for the ride.

———————

In order to be effective, a postwar Afghan government will have to be highly decentralized, a situation that had precedent in recent Afghan history prior to the Taliban's efforts to subjugate all self-governing non-Pashtun territories. A comment in that regard by Nazif Shahrani, professor of anthropology and Central Asian and Middle Eastern studies at Indiana University, is particularly appropriate:

The international community should encourage the creation of a government that recognizes the crucial

role of the local and regional communities in self-governance, as existed in earlier eras in Afghanistan.
Indeed, these kinds of local governing structures re-
emerged in the period of anti-Soviet and anti-Communist jihad during the 1980's and early 1990's. Areas
then controlled by mujahidin groups established rudi-
mentary governments that ran schools, police units
and courts; these local groups evolved into five major
regional coalitions of communities, consisting of several provinces each. The new government of Afghanistan should embrace the principles of community
self-governance at village, district and provincial lev-
els.

Local autonomy and the political integrity of every
ethnic and sectarian segment of Afghan society should
be guaranteed by a national constitution and a decentralized federal governance structure. [13]

At the same time that local autonomy should be
encouraged, ties between the central government and the
various regions should also be strengthened, both by a federal constitution and by practical measures such as
increased transportation links and commerce between
Kabul and the rest of the nation. Otherwise, the country
may fracture into the statelets that the international community is obligated to oppose.

What the international community must realize above
all is that putting together a postwar government involves
not merely trying to heal the wounds of the past two
decades. It means at the same time continuing the movement begun in earnest a generation ago of liberating the
nation from a barely extinguished feudalism that had
reigned for hundreds of years, with a few exceptions. The
two challenges cannot be separated. Respecting the past

does not mean repeating it; it means learning from it, and whenever possible, transcending it. The great traditions of Afghanistan are mixed in with the brutal ones. How could it be otherwise? It's the same in every country. Ben MacIntyre of *The Times* (London) once summarized the dark side of Afghan history when he said that it was one of "repeated invasion and permanent, chronic instability, compounded by internal tribal, ethnic and religious splits, coupled with an ancient warrior tradition, poverty, ignorance, corruption and multi-generational feuds buried so keep in the past that the roots have long been forgotten. The brutality of Afghanistan is matched only by its courage and its resilience."[14] To see the breadth of the challenge is one thing; one must also see its depth. A successful government in Afghanistan will glean the best of Afghan traditions and abandon the worst. It will allow religion its rightful place in Afghan society, but it will not allow theocratic despotism to rule.

Any good realtor will tell you that there are three criteria for assessing the value of a property: location, location, and location. The same criteria, though not exclusive, might apply for a student of geopolitics.

One has only to list the nations that touch Afghanistan's borders to understand why stability in Afghanistan is so important: Pakistan, Iran, China, Tajikistan, Uzbekistan, and Turkmenistan. And not far beyond Afghanistan's borders, in different directions, are Russia and India.

Two additional considerations, also related to geography, give Afghanistan importance far beyond its natural beauty: the poppy plant, oil, and gas. The mountainous climate of Afghanistan makes it amenable to poppy cultivation, and about 75 percent of the world's opium crop once came from Afghanistan. Who controls it and where it goes, licitly or illicitly, are political and economic matters. The fact that the poppy plant thrives in Afghanistan is climatic and geographic. That will not change, whoever is in charge. And it will continue to have international importance.

As for oil and gas, the significance of Afghanistan's location is in transport, not in natural resources. An article by Dominique Gallois and Marie Jego appearing in *Le Monde* stated that the zone of the Caspian Sea contained close to thirty billion barrels of proven oil and gas reserves, comparable in size to those of the North Sea. Those mineral reserves are concentrated among three countries of the former Soviet Union. Azerbaijan, Kazakhstan, and Turkmenistan. The reporters went on to say, "Since 1991, the region has become the center of a new 'great game' among the United States, Russia, and Iran for controlling the transport of hydrocarbons from the Caspian to European and Asian markets....Geopolitical tensions in the region concern as much the route of the proposed pipelines as ownership of the mineral resources."[15]

That same day, another story in *Le Monde*, this one by Richard Labévière, had this to say :

Chevron has invested 2 billion dollars in Kazakhstan, and controls 38% of the petroleum consortium in Azerbaijan. Washington has three principal objectives in the region: unconditional support for the sovereignty of post-communist states, its own economic interests, and the diversification of its energy sources. Toward that end, Washington convinced Turkey to accept the temporary isolation of Iran, and the rise in power of radical Islam (to combat communism) . . . Olivier Roy [an Afghan scholar] has said, *the petroleum companies have played a greater and greater role in the region. The seizure of power by the Taliban in Afghanistan in 1996 was largely orchestrated by the Pakistani secret service, and by the American petroleum company UNOCAL, which was allied with the Saudi company Delta.*[16]]

What these articles are claiming is that Washington, which once supported the mujahidin against the greater enemy of communism, is now concerned about the route that a needed pipeline will take to bring oil and gas from Central Asia to the rest of the world. Should it traverse or avoid Afghanistan? Needless to say, the economic and political stakes here are huge and go far beyond replacing the Taliban. A responsible Afghan government will have to deal with this issue.

January 2002

Notes

Preface

1. Najibullah, like many Afghans, used only one name. He had no surname. His popular nickname, obtained during his student days and based on his athletic prowess and build, was Najib-e-Gao, Najib the Bull. He was also known simply as Najib.
2. Report of the Secretary General, document A/47/705, 27 November 1992, paragraph 66.

1 Setting the Stage

1. Report of the Secretary General, document A/47/705, 27 November 1992, paragraph 13.
2. There are at least three books on the wars in Afghanistan from 1979 to 1992 that are indispensable for an understanding of the roots of those conflicts, and of the UN's efforts to bring peace to the region. They are: *The Search for Peace in Afghanistan: From Buffer State to Failed State* (New Haven, Conn.: Yale University Press, 1995) and *The Fragmentation of Afghanistan: State Formation and Collapse in the International System* (New Haven, Conn.: Yale University Press, 1995), both by Barnett Rubin; and *Out of Afghanistan: The Inside Story of the Soviet Withdrawal* (New York: Oxford University Press, 1995), by Diego Cordovez and Selig S. Harrison.
3. Although I identify all other personalities in this book by their last names, I will refer to Benon Sevan by his first name, because that is how I have always known him. It is also part of Benon's personality, even his style, to be familiar and accessible.
4. Cordovez and Harrison, *Out of Afghanistan*, 376–377.
5. Ibid., 368.
6. Rubin, *The Search for Peace in Afghanistan*, 89.
7. Cordovez and Harrison, *Out of Afghanistan*, 368.
8. Giandomenico Picco, *Man Without a Gun* (New York: Times Books, 1999), 17.
9. For elaboration of this idea, see my book *Dubious Mandate: A Memoir of the UN in Bosnia, Summer 1995* (Durham N.C.: Duke University Press, 1999).

10. Report of the Panel on United Nations Peace Operations, document A/55/305-S/2000/809, 21 August 2000.
11. Cordovez and Harrison, *Out of Afghanistan*, 4.
12. Ibid., 14.
13, Christopher Wren, "Afghanistan Opium Record Raises U,N, Fears," *New York Times*, 11 September 1999.
14. Barry Bearak, "At Heroin's Source, Taliban Do What 'Just Say No' Could Not," *New York Times*, 24 May 2001.
15. Michael R. Gordon and Erick Schmitt, "Afghanistan Remains a Major Drug Trader Despite Taliban Ban on Poppy Growing," *New York Times*, 26 September 2001.
16. Tim Weiner, "With Taliban Gone, Opium Farmers Return to Their Only Cash Crop," *New York Times*, 26 November 2001.

2 The Journal

1. M. Hassan Kakar, *Afghanistan: The Soviet Invasion and the Afghan Response, 1979–1982* (University of California Press, 1995), 274.
2. Cordovez and Harrison, *Out of Afghanistan*, 10.
3. Ibid., 161.
4. Ibid., 383–38.
5. Ibid., 10.
6. Picco, *Man Without a Gun*, discusses very intelligently the expanded role of the secretary-general following the end of the Cold War.
7. Three of the four previous leaders of Afghanistan had been murdered. The fourth had died in office. Sardar Mohammad Daoud, who had ousted his cousin and brother-in-law, King Zahir Shah, from power in 1973, was assassinated along with his family in 1978 during a military coup. His successor, Noor Mohammad Taraki, was suffocated less than a year later at the behest of his vice president, Hafizullah Amin, who was in turn murdered in 1979 by Babrak Karmal. Karmal came to power following the Soviet Union's invasion in December 1979. Karmal died in 1996 of cirrhosis of the liver and was succeeded by Najib.
8. Kakar, *Afghanistan*, 275.
9. Rubin, *The Search for Peace in Afghanistan*, 113.
10. Ibid., 114.
11. Kakar, *Afghanistan*, 275–276.

Epilogue

1. Resolution 1368.
2. As quoted by Stephen Kinzer in the *New York Times*, 1 December 2001.
3. Ibid.

4. UN document S/2001/1217, 19 December 2001.
5. An editorial in the *New York Times* on 20 December 2001 notes that "General Musharraf made a bold decision to side with the United States after Sept. 11. In return, Pakistan has been given more than $1 billion in loans and debt relief and is likely to benefit from the influx of aid to reconstruct Afghanistan."
6. Douglas Frantz, "Pakistan Ended Aid to Taliban Only Hesitantly," *New York Times*, 8 December 2001.
7. Dexter Filkins, "After Defeat, Journey to Uncertain Fate," *New York Times*, 28 November 2001.
8. Dexter Filkins and Carlotta Gall, *The New York Times*, November 24, 2001.
9. Erik Eckholm, "Still Heavily Armed, Ready to Die, and Recovering Nicely in War D," *New York Times*, 14 December 2001.
10. John Lee Anderson, "In the Court of the Pretender," *The New Yorker*, 5 November 2001.
11. Reuters, 22 December 2001.
12. An anonymous medical doctor, quoted by Anderson in "In the Court of the Pretender."
13. Nazif Shahrani, "Afghanistan Can Learn from Its Past," *New York Times*, 14 October 2001.
14. Ben MacIntyre, *The Times* (London), 5 October 2001.
15. Dominique Gallois and Marie Jego, "L'exportation des hydrocarbures, sujet stratégique majeur pour l'asie central," *Le Monde*, 5 October 2001. Translation by author.
16. Richard Labévière, "La course aux richesses pètrolières," Le Monde, October 20, 2001. Translation by author.

Selected Bibliography

United Nations Documents Cited in This Book

21 May 1991. SG/SM/4568-AFG/30. Appeal by secretary-general Javier Pérez de Cuéllar for further efforts to end suffering in Afghanistan.

27 September 1991. A/46/PV.7. Statement in General Assembly by prime minister of Afghanistan.

30 September 1991. A/46/PV.14. Statement in General Assembly debate by representative of Pakistan.

24 October 1991. A/46/595-S/23163. Text of joint statement by United States and Soviet Union on Afghanistan.

5 December 1991. A/RES/46/23. General Assembly resolution: "The situation in Afghanistan and its implications for international peace and security."

18 March 1992. A/47/128-S/23737. Statement by President Najibullah of Afghanistan.

19 March 1992. SG/SM/4718. Press conference by Secretary-General Boutros Boutros-Ghali.

10 April 1992. SG/SM/4728/Rev.1-AFG/43/Rev.1. Statement by secretary-general on agreement to establish pretransition council in Afghanistan.

16 April 1992. SG/SG/4731-AFG/44. Statement attributable to spokesman for Secretary-General Boutros Boutros-Ghali.

17 April 1992. A/47/165-S-23823. Statement by Republic of Afghanistan.

27 November 1992. A/47/705-S/24831. Report of the secretary-general on the situation in Afghanistan and its implications for international peace and security.

21 August 2000. A/55/305-S/2000/809. Report of the Panel on United Nations Peace Operations.

Other Sources

Arnold, Anthony. *Afghanistan's Two-party Communism: Parcham and Khalq.* Hoover Institution Press, Stanford University, 1983.

Boutros-Ghali, Boutros. *Unvanquished: A U.S.–U.N. Saga*. New York: Random House, 1999.

Brzezinski, Zbigniew. *Game Plan: A Geostrategic Framework for the Conduct of the U.S.–Soviet Contest*. New York: Atlantic Monthly Press, 1986.

Cordovez, Diego, and Selig S. Harrison. *Out of Afghanistan: The Inside Story of the Soviet Withdrawal*. New York: Oxford University Press, 1995.

Dupree, Louis. *Afghanistan*. Princeton, N.J.: Princeton University Press, 1978.

Grazda, Edward. *Afghanistan Dairy 1992–2000*. powerHouse Books, 2000.

Griffin, Michael. *Reaping the Whirlwind: The Taliban Movement in Afghanistan*. London: Pluto Press, 2001.

Harrison, Selig S. *In Afghanistan's Shadow: Baluch Nationalism and Soviet Temptations*. Washington, D.C.: Carnegie Endowment for International Peace, 1981.

Johnson, Chris. *Afghanistan: A Land of Shadow*. Oxford: Oxfam, 1988.

Juergensmeyer, Mark. *Terror in the Mind of God: The Global Rise of Religious Violence*. Berkeley: University of California Press, 2000.

Kakar, M. Hassan. *Afghanistan: The Soviet Invasion and the Afghan Response, 1979–1982*. Berkeley: University of California Press, 1995.

Khan, Riaz M. *Untying the Afghan Knot: Negotiating Soviet Withdrawal*. Durham, N.C.: Duke University Press, 1991.

Meyer, Karl E., and Shareen Blair Brysac. *Tournament of Shadows: The Great Game and the Race for Empire in Central Asia*. Washington, D.C.: Counterpoint, 1999.

Michener, James A. *Caravans*. New York: Random House, 1963.

Mousavi, Sayed Askar. *The Hazaras of Afghanistan: An Historical, Cultural, Economic and Political Study*. New York: Palgrave, 1997.

Netanyahu, Benjamin. *Fighting Terrorism: How Democracies Can Defeat the International Terrorist Network*, 2001 edition. New York: Farrar, Straus and Giroux, 1995.

Norval, Morgan. *Triumph of Disorder: Islamic Fundamentalism, The New Face of War*. Indian Wells, Calif.: Sligo Press, 1999.

Picco, Giandomenico. *Man Without a Gun: One Diplomat's Struggle to Free the Hostages, Fight Terrorism, and End a War*. New York: Times Books, 1999.

Rashid, Ahmed. *Taliban: Militant Islam, Oil and Fundamentalism in Central Asia*. New Haven, Conn.: Yale University Press, 2000.

Roy, Olivier. *Afghanistan: From Holy War to Civil War*. Princeton, N.J.: Darwin Press, 1995.

———. *The Failure of Political Islam*. Cambridge: Harvard University Press, 1994.

Rubin, Barnett R. *The Fragmentation of Afghanistan*. New Haven, Conn.: Yale University Press, 1995.
———. *The Search for Peace in Afghanistan: From Buffer State to Failed State*. New Haven, Conn.: Yale University Press, 1995.
Shawcross, William. *Deliver Us From Evil: Peacekeepers, Warlords, and a World of Endless Conflict*. New York: Simon and Schuster, 2000.

Index

Afghan Constitution, 67–68
Afghan expatriate A, 190
Afghan expatriates A and Z:
on Dostom's betrayal of
Najib, 192–193; on Dos-
tom's fear of fundamentalists, 193; on Dostom's
regrets, 194; on life under
Najib *versus* Taliban, 191;
on Najib's departure tim-
ing, 194–196; on UN peacekeeping mission in 1992,
191–192, 194–195; on
Yaqoubi's death, 193–194
Afghan expatriate Z, 190–191
Afghanistan, 189–190; Arab
mercenaries in, 76–77,
207–209; central authority
for, 202–203; Durand Line
and, 43–44; ethnic nationalism in, 17–18; ethnic rivalries in, 34, 44; foreign
troops in, 54–55, 205–206;
gender-sensitive govern-
ment in, 212–213; geopolitics of, 28–29, 216–218;
government negotiations
with Northern Alliance,
82–83; as host to international aid, 21; interim government in, 21; Iran and,
206; ISAF defeat of Taliban,
200–201; liberation from
feudalism in, 215–216; oil
and gas transport and, 216,
217–218; opium production
in, 30–32, 216–217; Pak-
istan and government of,
206–207; Pakistani merce-
naries in, 76–77, 207,
208–209; peacekeeping in,
22; post-Soviet withdrawal
agreements for, 19; postwar
decentralized government
for, 214–215; power vac-
uum in, 127–128, 200–201,
202; unified *versus* partitioned, 203–204; UN role
in, 59; urban-rural
dichotomy, 34–35; world
concerns about, 79. *see also*
Fazl-Ul-Haq-Khaliqyar;
Najibullah; refugees; Taliban
Afghans, as traders and warriors, 126
"Afghans abroad." *see* Afghan
expatriate A; Afghan expatriates A and Z; Afghan
expatriate Z; refugees
Ahmedzi, Shahpur, execution
of, *112*

on UN peacekeeping, 26.
see also Baker, James A.,
III; Baker–Pankin state-
ment; Bogue, Janet; Platt,
Nicholas
United States Central Command, UN peacekeepers
and, 205
UNOCAL (American oil com-
pany), 218
Uzbeks, 34, 73, *113*, 137–138.
see also Dostom, Abdul
Rashid

Vienna, Austria, as Loya Jirga
venue, 35–36, 37, 50
Vietnam war, 7
Voice of America, 125

Waheedullah, Statement of
the Republic of Afghani-
stan, 184–187; avoiding
personal responsibility in,
185–186; on mujahadin,
186, 187; on "political settlement," 186; on safety
and security of UN employees, 186–187
Wakil, Abdul, 70, 71–72, 127;
Najib and, 123; on Najib's
escape attempt, 114; post-
evacuation-attempt meet-
ing, 120–122; Sevan meets

with, 141–142; visits Sevan,
134
Waldheim, Kurt, 5
warlords, Afghan, 201–202;
as police authority,
202–203
Wassim, Canada House ser-
vant, 42
Watan (Homeland) Party, 82,
117–118. *see also* Layeq,
Sulaiman
Weiner, Tim, 32
Western culture, conflicting
attitudes toward, 40–41
Western Sahara, 4, 150
World Food Program, 32

Yaqoubi, Ghulam Faruq, 96,
110, 121, 193–194
Yar Mohammed, General,
81–84
Yeats, William Butler, 41, 65,
81
Yeltsin, Boris, 79
Yousaf, Mohammed, 47–48
Yugoslavia, 19, 26, 59. *see
also* Baker–Pankin state-
ment

Zahir Shah, King of Afghanistan, 38, 44, 213–214,
220n7
Zia Ul-Haq, 7–8, 10–11

About the Author

Phillip Corwin held a number of posts during his twenty-seven years with the United Nations, including that of a speechwriter for Secretary-General Javier Pérez de Cuéllar. During the 1990s, he served on peacekeeping missions in Western Sahara and throughout former Yugoslavia, as well as Afghanistan. While in the Department of Peacekeeping Operations at UN headquarters, he worked for Kofi Annan, who later became the UN's seventh secretary-general. Mr. Corwin's most recent book is *Dubious Mandate: A Memoir of the UN in Bosnia, Summer 1995* (Duke University Press, 1999). Since leaving the UN, Mr. Corwin has taken several assignments for the OSCE. He has been a political officer in Bosnia and an election monitor/supervisor in Kosovo and in the Ukraine. In addition to his political activities, he is a widely published poet and short story writer. He has taught fiction writing at New York University's School of Continuing Education and was a fellow at the Virginia Center for the Creative Arts.